Activism and the School Librarian

Activism and the School Librarian

Tools for Advocacy and Survival

Deborah D. Levitov, Editor

LIBRARIES UNLIMITED

AN IMPRINT OF ABC-CLIO, LLC
Santa Barbara, California • Denver, Colorado • Oxford, England

Library of Congress Cataloging-in-Publication Data

Activism and the school librarian : tools for advocacy and survival / Deborah D. Levitov, editor.
    pages cm
   Includes bibliographical references and index.
   ISBN 978-1-61069-187-1 (pbk.) — ISBN 978-1-61069-188-8 (ebook) (print)
1. School librarians—Professional relationships—United States.   2. School librarians—Political activity—United States.   3. School libraries—Aims and objectives—United States.   4. School libraries—United States—Marketing.   5. School libraries—Public relations—United States.   6. School libraries—Government policy—United States—Citizen participation.   7. Libraries and education—United States.   8. Libraries and community—United States.   9. Social advocacy.   I. Levitov, Deborah D.
   Z682.4.S34A28   2012
   027.80973—dc23   2012016873

ISBN: 978-1-61069-187-1
EISBN: 978-1-61069-188-8

16   15   14   13   12   1   2   3   4   5

This book is also available on the World Wide Web as an eBook.
Visit www.abc-clio.com for details.

Libraries Unlimited
An Imprint of ABC-CLIO, LLC

ABC-CLIO, LLC
130 Cremona Drive, P.O. Box 1911
Santa Barbara, California 93116-1911

This book is printed on acid-free paper ∞
Manufactured in the United States of America

For mentors—those people who give of themselves, their expertise, their time, and insight to help others learn, improve, and excel—and especially Dr. Clara T. Rottmann, former director of school libraries for Lincoln Public Schools, who encouraged me in my early years as a school librarian and provided many avenues for growth and leadership.

Contents

Figures

Introduction

Deborah D. Levitov

The definition of advocacy often falls in a gray area for school libraries. It is frequently associated with attributes equivalent to public relations and marketing, which for school libraries are seen as self-serving and motivated by the desire for job security. Thus the authors who contributed to this book decided to use the word *activism*. They felt activism better describes what school librarians must embrace when it comes to building strong programs and gaining the attention and support needed to keep school librarian positions and school library programs funded and staffed to meet the needs of 21st-century learners and teachers.

In the 1990s, I worked as coordinator for school libraries for a district that received a DeWitt-Wallace Reader's Digest Library Power grant. I worked with all schools in our district as they outlined and implemented their program goals for the grant. In the process, several school library programs emerged early as successful programs led by effective school librarians. These librarians knew what to do and how to do it when it came to building strong library programs linked to instruction. They were experts at developing strategies for outreach, communication, advocacy, and activism before these terms were key words for the profession. They were activists for the whole learning community and the library program, and they were central to its success. It was obvious that they had the skills and dispositions needed to thrive.

The pivotal role of the school librarian in program development and advocacy, shown by these Library Power participants, is not a new concept. There are many research studies (for example, Alexander and Carey 2003; Church 2010; Levitov 2009; Shannon 2002, 2009) that substantiate the school librarian as central to a successful and well-supported library. But often the success of such programs is not something that is undertaken in a deliberate or defined fashion; it seems to be based more on intuition. The message of this book is that it is crucial for all school librarians to consciously understand, define, and embrace the requirements for becoming one of these effective leaders and activists. In addition, the content provided in each chapter gives suggestions and solutions for accomplishing this goal.

The information offered in each chapter will help school librarians know how to build strong, exemplary plans for advocacy that will result in actions to sustain and support ongoing initiatives. The authors who contributed to this volume are an impressive, knowledgeable, and dedicated group of school library professionals who share invaluable expertise. The result is a one-of-a-kind book for all school librarians. There is no other book that has been published that offers this type of guidance for school librarians related to advocacy and activism.

The book begins with a chapter about professional dispositions by Gail Bush based on research she conducted in collaboration with Jami Jones. Through their research they have identified key characteristics that school librarians need to be successful—characteristics that are essential in building, driving, and sustaining school library programs (Bush and Jones 2010). These are characteristics that are easier and more natural for some, challenging and second nature for others, but they are attributes that *can* be acquired by all. They are *not* personality traits, but they are a prerequisite for viable school libraries that cannot be taken for granted.

Important dispositions needed by school librarians are reflected in every chapter of the book, and the reader will begin to see the importance of each. Chapter 1 offers the theoretical framework to serve as the base for chapters 2–7. Chapter 2 serves as a reminder that all advocacy should be linked to instruction, student learning, and assessment. Chapters 3–7 provide practical information that will assist school librarians in grappling with and finding solutions for the components of activism (such as proactive leadership, grassroots advocacy, legislative advocacy, school advocacy, and community advocacy).

The process of activism involves first understanding exemplary practice, having a vision for excellence in school library programming and a clear understanding of advocacy, and then developing a plan and putting it into motion, revisiting and revising it as needed. It requires the school librarian to identify and develop or strengthen personal attributes (dispositions) that will lead to success. It involves leading, making connections, communicating, collaborating, and educating on an ongoing basis.

This book is not about maintaining the status quo for school librarians or school libraries. Anyone who wants to garner support for the existence of school library programs or positions has to be willing to embrace the future and make changes that will transform and reinvent positions and programs, making them learner centered and essential for education in this century. This is an invitation to rethink and reimagine the roles, policies, infrastructure, and procedures that will create new and stronger school libraries and librarians while building advocacy plans that support that vision.

References

Alexander, L., and J. Carey. "Education Reform and the School Library Media Specialist: Perceptions of Principals." *Knowledge Quest* 32, no. 2 (November–December 2003): 10–13.

Bush, Gail, and Jami Jones. "Exploration to Identify Professional Dispositions of School Librarians: A Delphi Study." *School Library Media Research: American Association of School Librarians* 13 (May 2010). http://www.ala.org/ala/mgrps/divs/aasl/aaslpubsandjournals/slmrb/schoollibrary.cfm (accessed August 11, 2011).

Church, Audrey P. "Secondary School Principals' Perceptions of the School Librarian's Instructional Role." *School Library Media Research* 13 (2010). American Library Association, January 14, 2011. Document ID: 74f1589e-91de-9a74-8d3f-217badbbda24. http://www.ala.org/aasl/aaslpubsandjournals/slmrb/slmrcontents/volume13/church (accessed January 2, 2012).

Levitov, Deborah. *Perspectives of School Administrators Related to School Library Media Programs after Participating in an Online Course, "School Library Advocacy for Administrators."* PhD diss., University of Missouri–Columbia, 2009.

Shannon, Donna M. "Education and Competencies of School Library Media Specialists: A Review of the Literature." 2002. American Library Association, Document ID: 202809. http://www.ala.org/aasl/aaslpubsandjournals/slmrb/slmrcontents/volume52002/shannon (accessed January 2, 2012).

Shannon, Donna M. "Principals' Perspectives of School Librarians." *School Libraries Worldwide* 15, no. 2 (July 2009): 1–22.

Advocacy Definitions

Advocacy

On-going process of building partnerships so that others will act for and with you, turning passive support into educated action for the library program. It begins with a vision and a plan for the library program that is then matched to the agenda and priorities of stakeholders.

Public Relations (PR)

One-way communication of getting the message across.

- who we are
- what we do
- when and where
- and for whom

Marketing

A planned and sustained process to assess the customers' needs and then to select materials and services to meet those needs.

- know the customers' needs.
- who are they?
- what do they need?
- when and where can we best deliver it?
- what are you willing to pay? ($)

Definitions are from the American Association of School Librarians, Advocacy & Issues: Advocacy Definitions, http://www.ala.org/aasl/aaslissues/advocacy/definitions (accessed January 7, 2012).

1

The Promise of Library: A Theoretical Foundation for Activism

Gail Bush

What does *library* mean in the cacophony of American education? It is beyond the book report, research paper, and searching, beyond leisure reading, personal interests, and lifelong learning. It trumps Facebook, YouTube, and Twitter. It brushes off Wikipedia and Yelp like so much detritus.

To school librarians who are true believers, *library* is a concept, a state of becoming where inquiry becomes electric, questioning becomes eloquence, meaning becomes enlightenment, access becomes equanimity, advocacy becomes elegance, and activism becomes excellence. *Library* is a verb in the way that John Dewey describes the mind. We do library. Library is a disposition, a deliberate approach essential to life as we know it, impossible to live without, improbable to succeed otherwise.

What does library mean to our students, teachers, administrators, and parents? None of the above. And there is the rub. So you want to advocate for the promise of the school library, for what it can be for our students; you want to move policy makers to action. You are choosing activism as a path to influence societal change by way of the school library. You are not alone. The authors of this book are here to support your efforts doing what each of us does best. To provide a foundation upon which to build your argument, in this first chapter we are following psychologist Kurt Lewin's proclamation that "there is nothing so practical as a good theory" (Lewin 1951, 169).

To be politic about our deliberate steps toward the promise of library, we launch our discussion with a foundation steeped in basic human rights; a reflection of the power of context; a progressive perspective within the education field; a recognition of our place in social learning; and a look at diverse constructs of building knowledge. We conclude with professional dispositions that our students deserve from exemplary school librarians and that poise practitioners who are ready to advocate for a call to action.

Freedom to Achieve

Human Rights and the Capabilities Approach: Roosevelt and Sen

Although school library practitioners all act locally, our school community has a decidedly global impact. The International Federation of Library Associations's (IFLA) Standing Committee on School Libraries and Resource Centers supports a "One School, One Library" campaign; the International Association of School Librarianship recently partnered with the IFLA committee to publish a book on global perspectives of school librarianship (Oberg and Marquardt 2011). Supporting worldwide school library matters is a manifesto sponsored by UNESCO and a seminal document that was adopted by the United Nations on December 10, 1948.

Some might say that the crowning glory of Eleanor Roosevelt's tenure as first lady was her role as the champion of the development and adoption of the Universal Declaration of Human Rights. The entire document is an inspiration to free societies, but it is Article 19 that speaks most directly to school librarians worldwide. Article 19 proclaims that "Everyone has the right to freedom of opinion and expression; this right includes freedom to hold opinions without interference and to seek, receive and impart information and ideas through any media and regardless of frontiers" (UN General Assembly 1948).

Recognizing that access to education is a global economic and social justice concern brings the capabilities approach into the discussion. The capabilities approach focuses in its most basic form on "what people are actually able to do and to be" (Nussbaum 2003, 33). Nobel Prize winner for Economic Sciences Amartya Sen goes further to make a direct connection between poverty and education through the human capabilities approach theory. Although his earlier work included developing a theory of social choices, Sen later recognized capabilities as being "the substantive freedom of people to lead the lives they have reason to value and enhance the real choices they have" (1999, 293). He discusses "functionings" in his research that refer to the outcomes of capabilities. Sen essentially links the quality of education with access. His idea of functionings highlights educational access that utilizes a broad definition of access—physical access but also the ability to participate in a quality education (Dieltiens and Meny-Gibert 2008). Sen believes that education is transformative by taking our innate abilities and developing them into capabilities that in turn help us to live meaningful lives. The work of both Roosevelt and Sen provides a universal appeal to our global community that resonates in the depth and breadth of the school library. All children deserve open access to quality education and quality resources. This impact goes beyond the means of their studies to the development of their ends: their capabilities to have meaningful lives.

Reading the World

Critical Pedagogy and Situated Cognition: Freire and Lave

Brazilian critical pedagogist Paulo Freire's writings often focus on the politics of education, but they also admonish that we must learn to read the world so that we might read the word. We must be alert to the background for the text at hand, to be culturally and socially aware in every learning situation. As educators, we need to consider ourselves always incomplete, always becoming, and to understand the context within which we learn and our students learn. It seems that Freire holds to the ancient texts that teach us that the universe was created in a state of beginning and that it is for us to continue to complete it, to repair the universe. His is a hopeful message about our "unfinishedness" and being human with all the mystery and uncertainty that implies. Freire believes that education allows a person to understand that "though I know that things can get worse, I also know that I am able to intervene to improve them" (1998, 53).

Jean Lave's research supports the value of the authenticity of learning through the school library by proffering the critical importance of situated cognition (Brown, Collins, and Duguid 1989; Lave 1988). Lave claims that so much of doing school is in fact an artifice, that learning disciplines within the school structure are too far abstracted from the constructs essential to understanding the disciplines. Consider learning industrial arts without the shop, science without the lab, or physical education while sitting in a classroom. Lave's approach emphasizes the apprenticeship model of learning, which has a decidedly practical, applied, and action orientation. Although there are contrary views to Lave's research (Anderson, Reder, and Simon 1996, for example), the school library stands apart from the false constructs as identified by Lave and others and provides an authentic research laboratory designed to conduct actual research through access to resources relevant to any and all topics of study.

Read the teacher education literature and you will not often (if ever) see Freire and Lave brought together in the same breath, but somehow it makes sense through the lens of the school library as a learning environment. In his published conversations with Myles Horton, Freire says that "without practice there is no knowledge; at least it's difficult to know without practice" (Horton and Freire 1990, 98). The school library, as a learning laboratory, is a learning context that is not only available to students to practice research but is also consistently available throughout their tenure as students in the school—which could last up to nine (K–8) or thirteen (K–12) years over the life of a developing learner. Within the school context, what other learning environment has that potential power for access with developmentally appropriate scaffolding? Frankly, anything more than one year (185 days in many schools) is unusual for a teacher or a classroom experience to provide the power of context. But the school librarian and the library itself provide a context for situated cognition around learning and practicing research. The transfer problem that Lave identifies with the classroom does not exist in the research laboratory that is the school library. Inquiry in action in situ in the library, with skill sets smoothly transferring to the public library, is the very definition of learning as a lifelong, continuous enculturation process. Regardless of age, the researcher has a relational role in constructing and creating knowledge (Bredo 1994). The modern school library differs from other library facilities only through the appropriateness of the materials available to the ages of the students.

Freire (1998) takes the discussion further to connect education with the potential for social change. Again, the library as the context for the situated cognition is the ideal setting for researching action steps toward change. It is a place to inquire, maintain a critical stance, produce and distribute knowledge, and communicate with others to take social action. The call to action is louder to adolescents than to adults because change is a natural element in their ecosystem. The school librarian who masters the role of the "other," as Vygotsky describes, inspires more than a zone for development and might also influence the learner to prefer this model of facilitated learning.

Along this same vein, Albert Einstein defines education as

"that which remains, if one has forgotten everything he learned in school." The development of general ability for independent thinking and judgment should always be placed foremost, not the acquisition of special knowledge. If a person masters the fundamentals of his subject and has learned to think and work independently, he will surely find his way and besides will better be able to adapt himself to progress and changes than the person whose training principally consists in the acquiring of detailed knowledge. (Einstein 1950, 36)

Einstein does a nice job of describing the learning environment of the school library as an essential element of schools that are truly engaged in education.

A Footnote Encountered by Chance

Education as a Moral Responsibility: Dewey and Goodlad

Can you feel paradigms shift when there's hardly a breeze? If you are one of the prescient ones, perhaps you have your antennae up for school librarianship to move out from behind the shelves and into the center of learning. If you have an affinity for the notion of paradigms shifting, you can thank "a footnote encountered by chance" found by scientist Thomas Kuhn that discussed Piaget's experiments (1962, viii). Kuhn suggests that the Society of Fellows encouraged random exploration, which Kuhn took to heart. He claims to have spent much of his time exploring fields that were unrelated to his own. Alan Lightman, a physicist and author of *Einstein's Dreams*, recalls the "magic that cannot be replaced" when describing "what it feels like to unravel a mystery no one has understood before, sitting alone at my desk with only pencil and paper and wondering how it happened" (2005, 176). These scientists were schoolchildren once upon a time, and although we have an appreciation for the culture of learning and thinking in the classroom, we also have a responsibility for nurturing scholars in every field of study as we model learning dispositions through the school library. The better we are at cultivating a climate of critical thinking, creativity, and inquiry, the closer we come to the paradigm before us and, for the purposes of this discussion, the better we understand our purposes for advocacy and activism. At every turn, at every revelation and concept laid bare, we cannot limit this notion of the culture, climate, or resources of the school library to a physical space. Although space matters to us as communal beings, space is taking new meaning through emerging technologies, and the promise of library belongs in every learner's mind space, whatever form that might take.

The discourse presented throughout this chapter provides an educational context for what inevitably becomes the school librarian as the embodiment of the center of learning. It is the school librarian employing professional dispositions as advocate and activist for inquiry, for care of all students, and for teaching and learning through the school library. Why is there a focus on the school librarian? Because it is our solemn belief that this idea of library is our best response to John Dewey's stance as written in the 1959 publication *Moral Principles in Education*, which states,

> It is an absolute impossibility to educate the child for any fixed station in life. . . . The ethical responsibility of the school must be interpreted in the broadest and freest spirit; it is equivalent to that training of the child which will give him such possession of himself that he may take charge of himself; may not only adapt himself to the changes that are going on, but have the power to shape and direct them. (Dewey 1959, 11)

Having the power to shape and direct changes relates to the belief by school librarians that schoolchildren are not victims of their circumstances; that they may learn to take charge of themselves, and that the promise of library is an enduring catalyst to people who shape their own lives. And that the school library has a fundamental role in casting the dispositions that serve young people throughout their development of the life of the mind as they grow into thinking adults fully capable of personal choice and direction. The model of dispositions placed firmly within that context of the school library is the school librarian. The availability of an effective school library, including a qualified and mission-driven school librarian, is an undeniable right rather than a privilege in a democratic society dependent upon an informed electorate. And while this vision is certainly worthy of advocacy, it more profoundly impels school library activists to take action in speaking truth to power.

After all, where would all the political news conferences concerning education be filmed if it weren't for the school library? One particular video was shot in an elementary school library in Des Plaines, Illinois, in 1988. There are a few familiar faces in the room among the educators, including Dawn Heller, American Association of School Librarians (AASL) president in the making, wearing a vibrant red hat. Watching this videotape that was created to support the national guidelines published jointly by the American Association of School Librarians and the Association for Educational Communications and Technology Information Power is a revelation. It seems like another time and place until you start to listen to John Goodlad (of *A Place Called School* fame) talk about the school library and suddenly it feels as if you are listening to our universal message (1984). Goodlad implores us to recognize our moral obligation to our students. He talks about how students graduate from school but not from the library, how it is the library that connects them to the human conversation (AASL and AECT 1988).

Goodlad provides the attentive school library activist with impassioned and timeless messages throughout his work. His writing is very much like an ongoing conversation and is very accessible to the professional educator. Goodlad fleshes out his message in the Information Power video address in *In Praise of Education*, arguing,

> The educational challenge is to till and provide nutrients for fields of almost limitless human dreams. The fields are likely to be narrowly furrowed and sparsely planted when the goals are narrow, precise, and lacking in complexity. Selves do aspire to goals. But it is the journeys that inform and fulfill the self. Linear rationality that tightly joins means to ends narrows the scope of imagination and creativity. (Goodlad 1997, 149)

The Formation of the Self

Social Learning and Development: Bandura, Vygotsky, and Piaget

Unlike Paulo Freire and Jean Lave, social theorists Albert Bandura, Lev Vygotsky, and Jean Piaget are often grouped together under the cognitive development in the social world banner. Simply stated, Bandura posits that children develop through observing models, Vygotsky holds to the apprenticeship model, and Piaget believes that children learn independently even if it might be in the company of other children and that it is cognitive conflict that leads to development. Although clearly there are distinctions to be made among these theorists, it is their commonalities that are found in unanimously recognizing the role of the social world in development that clearly support the school library as an essential learning environment.

Countering the ubiquitous reading, packaged quizzes, and point systems, Bandura illuminated intrinsic rewards of learning as pride, motivation, and satisfaction (Bandura 1977). He considered this sense of accomplishment as an internal reward. His attention to internal thoughts and cognition while still nodding to the observation of models as a methodology of development explains the descriptions of his role as a bridge between the behaviorist and cognitive sciences. Bandura's social learning theory supports the school library as a place to observe models and to promote self-efficacy. More critically, however, is Bandura's recognition that observing behaviors does not necessarily motivate children to use those behaviors. The student-learning dispositions that are explicated in the AASL standards clearly involve not only being in possession of a learning behavior but also acting upon it in an appropriate and effective manner.

Play the association game in the education literature. Mention Vygotsky and you will immediately be bombarded with chants of "Z-P-D." The zone of proximal development (ZPD) as coined by Soviet social constructivist Lev Vygotsky is widely embraced as that supportive context whereby a learner progresses within a context of moving forward as modeled by another more developed learner. This "other" might be another student, a coach, teacher, resource educator, or perhaps a school librarian. The zone is that space between what is known by the student independently and what might be known with help from others (Vygotsky 1978, 86). The "other" in Vygotsky's sociocultural cognitive theory is referred to as the "more knowledgeable other" or MKO. Sadly, we rarely hear of the MKO even though the school librarian has effectively fulfilled that role for over a century. Taking a step further, we might suggest that within the learning context of the school library, there exist legions of authoritative MKOs within our resources—within the pages of our valid books and the screens of our vetted Web sites. Vygotsky was surely recognizing physically present others, but in the 21st century might he not identify those learned and generous bloggers, editors, and knowledge producers who are available to scaffold learning for our students?

Swiss development psychologist Jean Piaget, in contrast to both Bandura and Vygotsky, originally presented a more independent approach to cognitive development. The child interacts with the environment to work through the age-appropriate stage of development but not with others in the same manner that social learning theorists support. However, Piaget did acknowledge the role of the social environment as he continued to refine and edit his theories (Tudge and Winterhoff 1993). Discussion and argument with a peer played a part in helping the child to move beyond the preoperational stage. Piaget emphasized the role of the peer over the adult. The buddy reading programs and student tutoring programs are applications of Piaget's theories as well as those of Vygotsky and Bandura. It is very likely that it is the school library—with its flexible learning spaces, services, and programs—that finds a home for social learning theory in education today.

Social learning has taken on a broader definition since these cognitive development theories were established. Although the zone of proximal development defines the reach from the known to the next known, it might no longer exist purely within one physical learning space and time. The social interaction that Piaget came to recognize might be virtual as part of an online community. The peers that are so critical in Bandura's theory might be peers in a community that exists in a multiuser virtual environment and be avatars rather than persons in a physically communal space. The 21st-century school library brings along with it not only the core values of libraries, including access to resources and a service orientation to solving information problems, but also those learning theories that are sustained through the transition from traditional to emerging information media and processes. Social learning through the library is a dynamic building process that is fundamental to democratic knowledge societies. And the promise of libraries remains timeless and steady in the tsunami of information sea changes that seem to be engulfing our mission.

The Enterprise of Mind

Discovery and Mindfulness: Bruner and Langer

Cognitive psychologist Jerome S. Bruner has been an influence within the teaching for understanding Project Zero work at the Harvard University Graduate School of Education. He is most often associated with constructivism and most specifically with discovery learning, which he predicates on the work of John Dewey. In his collection of essays, *On Knowing: Essays for the Left Hand*, Bruner writes about discovery and Dewey in separate essays (1962). His discovery learning theory is constructivist at its base, with a focus on inquiry learning. Bruner believes that schools teach too much about what is known and not enough learning what is unknown. His discussions around the heuristics of inquiry are clear: Bruner proclaims that "of only one thing I am convinced: I have never seen anybody improve in the art and technique of inquiry by any means other than engaging in inquiry" (Bruner 1962, 94).

Writing "After John Dewey, What?" Bruner suggests that Dewey's focus on the social consciousness of the individual is a double-edged sword and that education both expands and limits our capabilities. From Bruner's perspective, education influences by giving us social experiences that are translated into our inner voices. And because education gives us that inner sound track, it could potentially "be the principal instrument for setting limits on the enterprise of the mind" (Bruner 1962, 117). Bruner then speaks to what we could all recognize as the promise of library: "The guarantee against limits is the sense of alternatives. Education must, then, be not only a process that transmits culture but also one that provides alternative views of the world and strengthens the will to explore them" (1962, 117). Access to resources, focus on inquiry, critical and creative thinking, and an abiding belief in the engagement of intellectual curiosity to best center learning supports the student who builds, produces, and shares knowledge.

Perhaps the promise of library pushes the limits of constructivism with a call to action through creating new constructs of the mind.

Mindfulness is a resounding response to this call that respects the boundaries of education as described by Bruner but expands our thinking beyond the standard enterprises of the mind. Ellen Langer, a Harvard University psychologist, has written extensively about mindful thinking, which is often confused with the age-old Eastern philosophy tenet. In Langer's research, mindfulness is described in contrast to intelligence. With intelligence, when we learn new information, we fit it into already formulated categories in our minds. The more we gather, the more we categorize, and the more intelligent we are.

When we are mindful, we view a situation from several perspectives with an open mind. We see the information presented as novel and attend to the context in which we are seeing it instead of making it fit into an established construct. Instead of choosing a best option for categorizing the new information, we create another option. Always new and fresh, we remain learners in touch with our novice selves. We create new categories through which we then understand the new information. Langer writes that the "ability to transcend context is the essence of mindfulness and central to creativity in any field" (Langer 1989, 131).

Educational psychologist Gavriel Salomon suggests that mindfulness includes "a positive attitude toward ambiguous and complex situations, a preference for novelty and incongruity, and an intention to seek out such situations, or even shape situations in a way that makes them fit the preference" (Salomon 1993). A textured example of this perspective allows for Thomas Kuhn being influenced by Piaget (see the Dewey and Goodlad section) and for Piaget claiming that he was inspired by Einstein's work on relativity when developing his theory on the child's conception of time. Consider that in the library we organize the world's knowledge and thereby are open to the information and ideas that are evident in the universe. We offer resources, space, and time to think, to make connections, and to see patterns emerge. The school library encompasses the mindful learning environment and reminds us that intelligence, when mindful, is not static but can grow and develop.

The World That Lay outside My Own

Professional Dispositions of School Librarians: Jones and Bush

In *Every Book Its Reader: The Power of the Printed Word to Stir the World*, bibliophile Nicholas Basbanes quotes Helen Keller who said that "circumscribed as my life was in so many ways, I had to look between the covers of books for news of the world that lay outside my own" (2005, 291). As unique as Keller's experience was, any self-respecting school librarian believes that it is his or her mission to both support the school curriculum and by doing so to expose students to the world that lays outside their own. We can feel it, the atmosphere of becoming, the sanctuary that honors and respects the learner both for who he or she is and for who he or she will be. We strive to provide the highest quality resources, services, and programs that further that mission. Inherently we know that each child can learn and that the school library holds promise for her brighter future. We, school librarians, (the choir) have believed, have felt, that is true but had no research to support these suppositions until 2009 when the authors developed a research agenda to explore the professional dispositions of exemplary school librarians (Bush and Jones 2010a, 2010b, 2011a, 2011b; Jones and Bush 2009a, 2009b, 2010). What we did have was our graduate experiences that oftentimes focused more on the warehousing and organizational aspects rather than the teaching and learning approach to school librarianship.

Following the launch of the AASL student learning standards in 2007 (AASL 2007), the authors found that the student learning dispositions had no antecedents in our field. If, as we learn from teacher education, dispositions are best learned through modeling, then practitioners needed to brush up on our dispositional selves, to "know thyself," and then perhaps we could model our student learning dispositions. Research conducted primarily in 2009 led to our findings of identified professional dispositions of exemplary school librarians. We requested that our expert scholar participants forecast what could be, not what they experienced in school libraries in the 20th century. We wanted to be forward thinking, to reach ahead and develop curriculum and signature pedagogies around what was recognized as exemplary.

The dispositions that were clearly the most highly regarded centered on teaching and reinforced the library as a learning environment. Descriptions that might resonate included: communicating respect of the learner, high expectations of learners, intellectually stimulating students, flexibility in teaching, responsive and differentiated instruction, and guided inquiry through evidence-based practices. Collaborating with educators was also highlighted, described as open communication and building partnerships for societal change and effective action. Leadership was described as a disposition of a visionary activist who leads by modeling and is honest, passionate, a change agent who has integrity, resilient, and a risk-taker. And lifelong learning was identified from the perspective of the practitioner as a learner who has a love of learning; an openness; an eagerness to continually explore emerging ideas, technologies, and professional trends; and who models curiosity and professional engagement. *Teaching, collaborating, leading,* and *learning* were the most noted dispositions in our research study.

The next set of dispositions, *creative thinking, empathy,* and *critical thinking,* when modeled, serve to provide an instructive framework for the school library as a learning environment. Creative thinking includes that genuine sense of wonder that innovative problem-finders share. Creative thinkers see opportunities where others feel cognitive dissonance; they seek novelty and find the questions in new information. Empathy is a powerful statement of compassion and care for each and every student that reinforces our mission to ensure that every student has equitable access to resources. We honor the diversity of our students and have openness to diverse perspectives; we are active and kind listeners. Critical thinking was described as an analytical, metacognitive, and strategic form of thinking, that disposition to delve into new ideas and to strive to stay ahead of change by being prepared for it.

Professionalism, ethics, advocacy, and *literacy* are also described as dispositions found to be important for exemplary school librarians. In further discussions about these dispositions, perhaps it would be useful to fully treat the advocacy disposition here. There is a sense among some expert scholars in the field that advocacy is redundant, that if all of the above-mentioned dispositions were in evidence, then advocacy would be unnecessary. Forecasting does not allow us to tell the future. Clearly advocacy of the promise of libraries is essential in order for us to have the luxurious experience of toying with the redundancy argument of advocacy. Descriptors that define the concept of advocacy as a professional disposition of school librarians included: communicative, positive, inherently optimistic, motivator, leading cheerleader, promotes, uses avenues that yield best results, encourages individual pursuits, creates coalitions, and maintains relationships. As advocacy within the library field is viewed primarily as the ongoing process of many of these descriptors, it behooves us to pursue this disposition as the foundation of school library activism.

The process of advocacy in action, or activism, is the subject of the following chapters of this book. This theoretical foundation gives us a power of contextual thinking around issues and perspectives that are realized by the promise of library. Certainly some theories might resonate more or less with each individual school experience and learning environment. We are hopeful that the language, theories, and historical context will ground us and will answer the "why" question that will inevitably be asked of the school library activist who takes this mission of the promise of library to heart. Invite the question; be confident in your response.

References

American Association of School Librarians and Association for Educational Communications and Technology. *Information Power: Guidelines for School Library Media Programs.* VHS. Frank Frost Productions, Encyclopedia Britannica Educational Corp., 1988.

"American Association of School Librarians Standards for the 21st-Century Learner." *American Library Association.* www.ala.org/ala/mgrps/divs/aasl/guidelinesandstandards/learning standards/AASL_Learning_Standards_2007.pdf (accessed October 3, 2011).

Anderson, John R., Lynne M. Reder, and Herbert A. Simon. "Situated Learning and Education." *Educational Researcher* 25, no. 4 (May 1996): 5–11.

Bandura, Albert. *Social Learning Theory.* Englewood Cliffs, N.J.: Prentice-Hall, 1977.

Basbanes, Nicholas A. *Every Book Its Reader: The Power of the Printed Word to Stir the World.* New York: HarperCollins, 2005.

Bredo, Eric. "Cognitivism, Situated Cognitivism, and Deweyian Pragmatism." *Philosophy of Education 1994.* Philosophy of Education Society Yearbook (1994): 47–56.

Brown, John S., Allan Collins, and Paul Duguid. "Situated Cognition and the Culture of Learning." *Educational Researcher* 18, no. 32 (1989): 32–42.

Bruner, Jerome S. *On Knowing: Essays for the Left Hand.* Cambridge, Mass.: Harvard University Press, 1962.

Bush, Gail, and Jami L. Jones. "Exploration to Identify Professional Dispositions of School Librarians: A Delphi Study." *School Library Media Research: American Association of School Librarians* 13. May 2010a. http://www.ala.org/ala/mgrps/divs/aasl/aaslpubsandjournals/slmrb/schoollibrary.cfm (accessed August 11, 2011).

Bush, Gail, and Jami L. Jones. "Forecasting Professional Dispositions of School Librarians." *School Library Monthly* 27, no. 4 (January 2011a): 54–56.

Bush, Gail, and Jami L. Jones. "Revisiting Professional Dispositions." *School Library Monthly* 28, no. 2 (November 2011b): 14–16.

Bush, Gail, and Jami L. Jones. *Tales Out of the School Library: Developing Professional Dispositions.* Santa Barbara, Calif.: Libraries Unlimited, 2010b.

Dewey, John. *Moral Principles in Education.* New York: Philosophical Library, 1959.

Dieltiens, Veerle, and Sarah Meny-Gibert. "Poverty, Equity and Access to Education." Southern African Comparative and History of Education Society (SACHES) annual conference paper, Wits Education Policy Unit and Social Surveys Africa, Maputo, Mozambique, July 17–19, 2008.

Einstein, Albert. *Out of My Later Years*. New York: Philosophical Library, 1950.

Freire, Paulo. *Pedagogy of Freedom: Ethics, Democracy, and Civic Courage*. Lanham, Md.: Rowman and Littlefield, 1998.

Goodlad, John I. *A Place Called School: Prospects for the Future*. New York: McGraw-Hill, 1984.

Goodlad, John I. *In Praise of Education*. New York: Teachers College Press, 1997.

Horton, Myles, and Paulo Freire. *We Make the Road by Walking: Conversations on Education and Social Change*. Philadelphia: Temple University Press, 1990.

Jones, Jami, and Gail Bush. "Dispositions of Exemplary School Librarians: How Professional Dispositions Relate to Student Learning in the 21st Century." In *Preparing Pupils and Students for the Future: School Libraries in the Picture—Selected Papers from the 38th Annual Conference of the International Association of School Librarianship, and the Thirteenth International Forum on Research in School Librarianship*, Abano Terme, Padua, Italy, 2–4 (September 2009a).

Jones, Jami, and Gail Bush. "Towards an Understanding of Professional Dispositions of Exemplary School Librarians." In *Educational Media and Technology Yearbook*, ed. Michael Orey et al., 35. Littleton, Colo.: Springer, 2010.

Jones, Jami, and Gail Bush. "What Defines an Exemplary School Librarian? An Exploration of Professional Dispositions." *Library Media Connection* 28, no. 6 (2009b): 10–12.

Kuhn, Deanna. *Education for Thinking*. Cambridge, Mass.: Harvard University Press, 2005.

Kuhn, Thomas. *The Structure of Scientific Revolutions*. Chicago, Ill.: University of Chicago Press, 1962.

Langer, Ellen J. *Mindfulness*. New York: Perseus Books, 1989.

Lave, Jean. *Cognition in Practice*. Cambridge: Cambridge University Press, 1988.

Lewin, Kurt. "The Research Center for Group Dynamics at Massachusetts Institute of Technology." *Sociometry* 8, no. 2 (1951): 126–35.

Lightman, Alan. *A Sense of the Mysterious: Science and the Human Spirit*. New York: Vintage, 2005.

Nussbaum, Martha C. "Capabilities as Fundamental Entitlements: Sen and Social Justice." *Feminist Economics* 9, no. 2–3 (2003): 33–59.

Oberg, Dianne, and Luisa Marquardt (eds.). *Global Perspectives on School Libraries: Projects and Practices*. International Federation of Library Associations, 2011.

Salomon, Gavriel. *Distributed Cognitions*. Cambridge: Cambridge University Press, 1993.

Sen, Amartya. *Development as Freedom*. New York: Alfred A. Knopf, 1999.

Tudge, Jonathan R. H., and Paul A. Winterhoff. "Vygotsky, Piaget, and Bandura: Perspectives on the Relations between the Social World and Cognitive Development." *Human Development* 36 (1993): 61–81.

UN General Assembly. *Universal Declaration of Human Rights*, December 10, 1948, 217 A (III). http://www.unhcr.org/refworld/docid/3ae6b3712c.html (accessed September 2, 2011).

Vygotsky, Lev S. *Mind and Society: The Development of Higher Mental Processes*. Cambridge, Mass.: Harvard University Press, 1978.

Additional Resources

Bandura, Albert. *Social Foundations of Thought and Action*. New York: Prentice-Hall, 1986.

Bruner, Jerome S. "Celebrating Divergence: Piaget and Vygotsky." Keynote address, joint meeting of the "Growing Mind Conference" in honor of the centennial of Piaget's birth, and the "Vygotsky-Piaget Conference" of the Second Congress of Socio-Cultural Research, Geneva, Switzerland, September 15, 1996.

Center for Inspired Teaching: Students, Teachers, and Schools Achieving Their Full Potential. "Inspired Issue Brief: Inquiry-Based Teaching." Washington, D.C.: Center for Inspired Teaching, 2008.

D'Addelfio, Giuseppina. "The Educative Value of Empathy within the Capability Approach." Unpublished paper, Dipartimento di Filosofia, Storia e Critica dei Saperi, University of Palermo, Italy.

Dewey, John. *Democracy and Education: An Introduction to the Philosophy of Education*. New York: Macmillan, 1916.

Dewey, John. *How We Think*. New York: D. C. Heath, 1910.

Dewey, John. *Human Nature and Conduct*. New York: Modern Library, 1922.

Feinberg, Cara. "The Mindfulness Chronicles: On 'The Psychology of Possibility.'" *Harvard Magazine* (September–October 2010): 42–45.

Giroux, Henry A. *Teachers as Intellectuals: Toward a Critical Pedagogy of Learning*. Granby, Mass.: Bergin and Garvey, 1988.

hooks, bell. *Teaching to Transgress: Education as the Practice of Freedom*. New York: Routledge, 1994.

Jackson, Philip W. *Untaught Lessons*. New York: Teachers College Press, 1992.

Kirschner, Paul A., John Sweller, and Richard E. Clark. "Why Minimal Guidance During Instruction Does Not Work: An Analysis of the Failure of Constructivist, Discovery, Problem-Based, Experiential, and Inquiry-Based Teaching." *Educational Psychologist* 41, no. 2 (2006): 75–86.

Langer, Ellen J. *The Power of Mindful Learning*. New York: Perseus Books, 1998.

Mardis, Marcia. "Introduction: A Gentle Manifesto on the Relevance and Obscurity of School Libraries in LIS Research." *Library Trends* 58, no. 1 (Summer 2009): 1–8.

Neuman, Delia. "Research in School Library Media for the Next Decade: Polishing the Diamond." *Library Trends* 51, no. 4 (Spring 2003): 503–24.

Nieto, Sonia. *The Light in Their Eyes: Creating Multicultural Learning Communities: 10th Anniversary Edition*. New York: Teachers College Press, 2009.

Postman, Neil, and Charles Weingartner. *Teaching as a Subversive Activity*. New York: Delacorte Press, 1969.

Unterhalter, Elaine, Rosie Vaughan, and Melanie Walker. "The Capability Approach and Education." *Prospero* 13, no. 3 (November 2007): 13–21.

2

Teaching and Learning: The Heart of Advocacy

Deborah D. Levitov

Students . . . are the chief users of the library and the sole reason for its existence.

—P. H. Anderson, 1990

Before reading the remaining chapters of this book, school librarians should stop and realize that advocacy planning and activism can only be successful when student learning is at the heart of every advocacy plan conceived, created, and acted upon for school libraries. As Carol Tilley so aptly states,

> School librarians will be safe from decimation only when all of them focus their message and efforts on kids, not the physical space and not the profession. The real value of the work of school librarians can be measured by the impact the school library program has on the lives of the children in schools. (Tilley 2011, 46)

This was a realization that also became clear for school librarians organizing the Pennsylvania School Library Association (PSLA) legislative campaign:

> Prior to HR 987, PSLA tried to clarify the role of the librarian, often recanting that the mission of the school library is "to ensure that students and staff are effective users of ideas and information" (American Association of School Librarians 2009, 8). *It became clear the message needed to be about equality of services for students, not just about what school librarians do.* No parent or legislator wants to hear that their children or constituents are at an educational disadvantage due to inequities of resources. The revised message changed the focus from public relations (who librarians are and what they do) to a marketing message (what librarians can do for you). So now the message is: *Ensure that all Pennsylvania's K–12 students have access to quality school library programs with a certified school librarian who teaches 21st-century learning skills.* (Kachel 2011; emphasis added)

The work of school librarians, along with the focus of school library programs, must be based on what is best for students, what will help them learn and learn in a meaningful way. "The purpose of the school library is to cause student learning" and school librarians are "on the cutting edge" to do just this (Zmuda 2010, 6).

Advocacy built on this concept is what is needed to show the value of school libraries. It is what is meant by Buffy Hamilton when she urges the assessment of student learning and the reframing of the school librarian as a learning specialist: "Good library business is about plotting and sticking to the library's commitment to student learning" (Hamilton 2011). At the heart of accomplishing advocacy for school libraries is evidence-based practice and assessment. It is a topic that challenges the school library profession and one that individual school librarians often dance around and away from. That avoidance is understandable because assessment and evidence of student learning is not easily accomplished. But it is what is needed; it is essential for meaningful advocacy that resonates with stakeholders.

Learning Specialists

Advocacy described in this book will be most effective when data and evidence are used to show why the message is important to student learning and thus to parents, legislators, community members, school board members, classroom teachers, and administrators. Evidence showing how school librarians and school library programs affect student learning is the most challenging to gather, yet it is the most crucial proof needed to garner support that will legitimize and ensure the ongoing existence of school libraries, staffed by certified librarians. It provides an opportunity to combine the roles for school librarians outlined in the American Association of School Librarians guidelines for school libraries: leader, instructional partner, information specialist and teacher, and program administrator into that of the learning specialist. The learning specialist is a professional who "can facilitate the growth of school teams that truly support one another to make the sharing of expertise part of the culture of teaching"; they are "strategically positioned to be teacher leaders" (Zmuda and Harada 2008a, xvi).

When urging school librarians to claim their authority, Allison Zmuda argues that authority comes from identifying and substantiating the achievement gap, "the chasm between the academic expectations for learners and the current achievement levels of students within the school" (2006, 19). In her article "Where Does Your Authority Come From? Empowering the Library Media Specialist as a True Partner in Student Achievement," Zmuda offers strategies for gathering data, assessing practice, and assessing student learning (see pages 19–22). This is a call for school librarians to examine practice and to change and improve instruction as well as services and resources of the school library program—the role as teacher. This type of work will provide the strongest and most meaningful form of advocacy.

The work of the school librarian should begin with the following questions: "What am I here for? What are my students here for?" (Zmuda 2006, 20). The authority of a school librarian is derived from identifying and addressing the achievement gaps related to skills and from understanding what is needed by students to be successful to meet the demands of the workplace in the 21st century (Zmuda 2006, 19). School librarians can begin by using simple devices such as Zmuda's rubric, "Use This Page: Student Learning in the Library Media Center: What am I here for? What are my students here for?" which can be used to track and record work done with classroom teachers to focus instructional practice and meet student learning needs (see page 23).

Moving away from bad business where...	Moving toward good business where...
Success is defined by the number of staff who collaborate with the library media specialist.	Success is defined by the quality of the work completed in the library media center.
Success is defined by doing whatever is asked in order to be recognized as valuable or important.	Success is defined by investing resources only in those tasks that are central to the library mission.
Success is defined by helping students find what they are looking for.	Success is defined by engaging students in the construction of deep knowledge through the exploration of ideas and information, conducting of investigations, and communication and evaluation of findings.
Success is defined by the number of instructional sessions held in the library media center.	Success is defined by the student learning that resulted from completion of work centered on subject area and information literacy goals.

Fig. 2.1.   Bad and good business practices for school librarians. (Zmuda and Harada 2008b, 43)

Becoming a learning specialist by directly contributing to the achievement of all learners will provide school librarians with the ability to define "good business" in the school library and move away from "bad business" (Zmuda and Harada 2008b, 43); see figure 2.1. This will require data collection and analysis that show what the school librarian does on a daily basis (instruction, collection development, and so forth) and how it has the desired effect on student learning (Zmuda and Harada 2008b, 46). The result of "good business" will be

> the sound of students engaged in the construction of knowledge and the communication of thinking, the opportunity to see that the investment of resources positively affects student performance on higher-order tasks and staff teaching practices, and the sense of satisfaction that the library is the most information-rich, inquiry-rich, resource-rich, pedagogically-rich classroom in the building. (Zmuda and Harada 2008b, 46)

Instructional Practice and Assessment

School librarians have access to many available resources for addressing assessment and gathering evidence, as well as improving instructional practice in a way that places priority on meaningful student learning. Also available are excellent tools to help school librarians gather the proof needed to link school library programs and librarians to students learning. The following is a short list of authors and excellent resources as well as online tools. Other resources can be found listed in the References and Additional Resources list at the end of this chapter.

- Donham provides strategies for assessing instructional design with the goal of determining that assignments are worth doing (2011, 5–7). All school librarians need to embrace the challenge presented in Donham's chart "Guide to deep learning through inquiry" (see figure 2.2, page 16).
- Marjorie L. Pappas provides specific guidelines for designing learning for evidence-based practice and advice for gathering and recording evidence; see

Deep Learning and Inquiry

Criteria	How does this project measure up?	How can it be improved?
Concept-based 1. Does it demand students sustain a focus on a significant concept? 2. Does it require engagement in higher-order thinking? 4. Is the outcome of the project insight or only information?		
Application to Real-World 1. Does the project emanate from a problem or question that has meaning to the student? 2. Must students adopt a critical stance in evaluating found information and applying it to the problem at hand? 2. Must students develop organizational skills and social responsibility in using information? 3. Does the project lead students to acquire and use competencies in teamwork and/ or problem-solving?		
Substantive technology Integration 1. Does the use of technology deepen the learning 2. Does the technology afford opportunities for learning not otherwise possible? (beyond creativity or motivation?)		
Active Intellectual Exploration 1. Must students generate a cognitively complex research question? 2. Does the task require students to engage in integrating a variety of information resources? 3. Must students integrate prior knowledge and new learning to arrive at new understandings? 4. Are students expected to communicate what they are learning to an identified audience?		

Fig. 2.2.   Guide to deep learning through inquiry. (Donham 2011, 6)

the appendix, page 100, for the chart "Use This Page: Designing Learning for Evidence-Based Practice" (Pappas 2008, 2, 19–23). Pappas also describes many approaches to assessment, such as student logs, checklists, rating scales, organizers, matrices, concept maps, webs, and rubrics (2007, 22). The information gathered provides evidence of learning; "Used in conjunction with the evidence gathered by classroom teachers, library media specialists can show how the library media program supports the content standards and student achievement" (Pappas 2007, 24).

- Vi Harada offers practical guidance for school librarians through a long list of articles (see References and Additional Resources) that drill into learning assessment, as does Harada and Joan Yoshina's book, *Assessing for Learning* (2010), an invaluable resource for improving instructional practice and determining assessments for student learning.

- Carol Kuhlthau et al. also offer solutions in the form of student surveys through *Guided Inquiry* (2007). Kuhlthau's work is the basis for the Student Learning through Inquiry Measure (SLIM) toolkit featured in "Online Resources for Assessment of Student Learning Assessment."

- Barbara Stripling provides understanding of inquiry in her article "Inquiry: Inquiring Minds Want to Know" (Stripling 2008) and the role of the school librarian related to teaching in learning. (See appendix, page 101, for "Use This Page: Inquiry-based Teaching and Learning—The Role of the Library Media Specialist" (2008, 50–52.)

- Other specific resources that will be helpful for school librarians include Harada and Zmuda, "Reframing the Library Media Specialist as a Learning Specialist" (2008); Jean Donham, *Enhancing Teaching and Learning: A Leadership Guide for School Library Media Specialists* (2008); and Virginia Wallace and Whitney Norwood Husid, *Collaborating for Inquiry-Based Learning: School Librarians and Teachers Partner for Student Achievement* (2011).

Online Tools for Assessment of Student Learning

- *Tool for Real-Time Assessment of Information Literacy Skills* (TRAILS) is another resource available to school librarians to help assess student knowledge of information literacy skills based on 3rd-, 6th-, 9th-, and 12th-grade standards. TRAILS was developed as a tool to identify strengths and weaknesses in the information-seeking skills of students (http://www.trails-9.org/).

- *Student Learning through Inquiry Measure* (SLIM) toolkit is available from the Center for International Scholarship in School Libraries (CISSL) Web site (http://cissl.rutgers.edu/impact_studies.html). It includes the SLIM Reflection Instruments and Scoring Guidelines, SLIM Handbook, and SLIM Scoring Sheet. "The documents provide the rationale and step-by-step processes for implementing the assessment instruments, for engaging with and analyzing the data, for constructing claims about student learning, and for disseminating the findings" (Todd 2011, 8).

- *Student Surveys* from the Center for Digital Literacy (http://digital-literacy .syr.edu/site/view/80) are used to assess motivational aspects of middle school children's information-seeking and digital-technology skills.

Focusing on Program Improvement

It is important to differentiate between evidence-based instructional strategies and evidence-based program evaluation (Callison 2007, 45), but program evaluation and assessment is a sensible and manageable way to improve instruction and gain focus for evidence-based practice with well-structured goals. It is a way to examine what is being done and to set goals for improvement.

Allison Zmuda outlines a set of six steps to save school libraries that focuses on the importance of quality, authentic learning for students through examination of the library program mission statement, program alignment, student learning, quality tasks, instructional time, and understanding cognition (2011, 45–48); see the appendix, page 102, for the chart "Use This Page: Taking Action: Saving School Libraries: Six Steps: Saving Your Library Program."

Developing simple devices to record the work related to individual instructional units conducted with classroom teachers is a way to gather data that will identify successes and gains as well as possible gaps in collaborative undertakings (Zmuda 2006); see the appendix, page 103, for "Use This Page: Assessment Tool: Levels of Communication, Cooperation, and Collaboration with Teachers." The results can be summarized and then shared with administrators to show work done over the course of a school year. This type of tool, combined with tools that assess learning and research objectives, will begin to help school librarians accrue the type of evidence needed to show student learning as the basis for advocacy. See "Use This Page: Assessing the Research Proccess: Rubric for Assessing the Research Objectives" in the appendix, page 104, and "Use This Page: Planning and Assessing Inquiry-based Learning" in the appendix, page 105.

Also available to school librarians are tools developed specifically for program evaluation and assessment. These resources can be used to focus program goals on instructional practice that incorporates a learning assessment focus.

- American Association of School Librarians: *A Planning Guide for Empowering Learners with School Library Program Assessment Rubric* (available from http:// aasl.eb.com/planningGuideForEmpoweringLearnersController.htm)
- Colorado State Libraries: *School Library Program Competencies—Evaluation Rubric* (available from http://www.cde.state.co.us/cdelib/powerlib/download/ SchoolLibraryEvalRubric.pdf)
- New York State Education Department: *School Library Media Program Evaluation (SLMPE) Rubric* (available from http://www.p12.nysed.gov/technology/ library/SLMPE_rubric/)

In Summary

The expertise of the school librarian differs from that of the classroom teacher. The school librarian is allowed a broad perspective of the school and education, is a teacher who can offer leadership related to instructional design and assessment, and is an in-

Where Does Your Authority Come From?

Empowering the Library Media Specialist as a True Partner in Student Achievement

by Allison Zmuda

The library media center has long been a beloved and specialized learning environment for students, a place rich with opportunities to pursue specialized inquiries, interests, and ideas. It is the most natural venue in schools for differentiation, integration of technology, and collaboration. In recent years, state and national standards for information literacy and technology have delineated a framework for what students are expected to know and be able to do as a result of their work in the library media center. Noted education researchers, system leaders, and authors as well as foundations have further bolstered the importance of the library media center as an integral part of 21st century learning so that students are prepared for the demands of the workplace. There has never been a more exciting or potentially powerful time to be a library media specialist.

There is, however, one fundamental problem that has existed for years and has frustrated specialists for years: How do we get the authority to teach students? If they don't come to the library media center at all or come for a meaningful purpose (i.e., a task where students are expected to work in critical and creative ways to collect, analyze, and synthesize information), then how can students be expected to achieve the standards?

True authority does not come from the superintendent, principal, or even the teachers worked with every day; it comes from a very large achievement gap. This achievement gap is the chasm between the academic expectations for learners and the current achievement levels of students within the school. Most specialists have been aware of this gap for years and many have vocalized those concerns and, consequently, lobbied for broader access to students and more resources. The major stumbling block, however, is that without data to illustrate this gap, it looks like a rhetorical contention based on the unabashedly biased viewpoint of those professionals that seem to have the most to gain. So, to claim the authority needed to close this achievement gap, it is important to get the data to show the current student achievement levels, compare that to state/national standards for learning, and then propose short-term

Allison Zmuda is an Educational Consultant with Education Connection in Litchefield, CT. She was the keynote speaker at the Treasure Mountain Research Retreat #12, Pittsburgh, PA, October 2005. Email: azmuda@hughes.net and long-term ways to close those gaps.

What kind of data are we talking about?

A reliable measure of student achievement requires getting a collection of different types of evidence. For example, the amount of time a student has spent in the library media center is a necessary, but not sufficient, piece of information because seat time alone is not a predictor of learning success.

> **Questions to guide the data collection process:**
> 1. What do we have to find out?
> 2. What data are currently available?
> 3. What new data do we need?
> 4. How do we obtain data?
> 5. How can we collect data in a valid and reliable form?
>
> **Guidelines to support the effort:**
> • Measure what is necessary, not what is convenient
> • Keep focused on what is being evaluated: student learning, not individual educators
> • Involve key stakeholders in dialogue about the intent of the data collection process (before, during, and after)
> • Involve staff in the collection and analysis
> • Use data to produce a collective mandate for change

Examples of powerful data sources include:
- Existing information literacy requirements (how much time students at each grade level are required to be in the library media center and the focus of that requirement—orientation vs. development),
- Analysis of state content standards in all subject areas to determine how many require information and technology literacy,
- Required core assessments completed by all students in a grade level/course to evaluate incorporation of information and technology literacy,
- Daily attendance figures in the library media center (also accounting for how many times the center was full which limited the use for others)
- Percentage of teachers who bring students to the library 0-2, 3-5, and 6+ times per year,
- Nature of the tasks students are working on (i.e., classify by level on Bloom's taxonomy).

Now that I have the attention of the staff, what do I do next?

Once the preliminary data is collected and communicated, the next challenge is how to act on that information in a way that enlists the support of classroom teachers and leaders to raise student achievement. It is critical to keep the focus on the results so that staff see subsequent actions (both on a daily basis and in long-term planning) as a necessary means to achieve the desired end. Whatever the status quo currently looks like (nature of relationships with teachers, existing resources, level of support from school, system, and state leaders), two conditions must be met to positively impact student achievement:
- Library media specialists view every point of contact with a teacher and his/her respective students as a true collaboration of content areas.
- Library media specialists view the collection, analysis, and reflection on student achievement data as a primary part of their work.

Condition #1: Library media specialists view every point of contact with a teacher and his/her respective students as a true collaboration of content areas.

Collaboration rooted in trust and respect among committed adults is the most essential condition for meaningful change in any organization. "Without trust and respect, there is no real learning and dialogue about the need for change" (Wagner 1997, 29). The library media specialist must never sacrifice the opportunity to develop information literacy skills just to pacify or cajole a teacher to come to the library media center. Not only does this deference diminish student clarity about what research and synthesis involves, but also relegates the specialist to a supporting role instead of a meaningful partner in the professional learning community. Specialists must communicate the vision and expectations for student learning in the library media center so that teacher and student alike are clear on what is expected when they work in this environment. (See Figure 1).
- When staff come together to

Figure 1
(See reproducible on page 2).

Student Learning in the Library Media Center What am I here for? What are my students here for?		
Basic Task Description	Individual/Teacher Expectations	Areas of Information Literacy (check those that apply)
		☐ Define and clarify ☐ Locate and retrieve ☐ Select, process, and record data ☐ Analyze ☐ Synthesize ☐ Share and use ☐ Reflection
What areas of Information Literacy are new for you/your students?		
What areas do you/your students have experience in but still may have questions about?		
What areas do you/your students have a lot of experience and success in?		

work on any task, they must first be clear about what they are doing and why they are doing it. This provides the opportunity for classroom teacher and library media specialist to envision what the student learning outcomes will be, thus creating potent internal accountability. (See Figure 2.)

• Teamwork is not something that should be talked to death upfront—it can happen quickly if teachers are required to do the work together and the success of the work is measured by the established outcomes.

• Staff should be expected to "surface problems to which they have no immediate solutions" so that the organization can learn (Elmore 2005). This requires more than complaining about a concern; it requires that each issue be collectively scrutinized to identify root causes and possible action steps. Once action steps are identified, both teacher and specialist understand what they are supposed to do and how those actions will impact the work of the team.

The legacy of these opportunities is that members of the staff come to trust that the increased capacity they have together eclipses their best individual efforts. They not only see the powerful connections that already bind them together, but work much more proactively to maximize the power of these connections.

Condition #2: Library media specialists view the collection,

Figure 2: Nature of Teacher/Library Media Specialist Collaboration

	Isolated Event	Coordinated Effort	Partnership
Design	Teacher approaches library media specialist to reserve space in the library for students to complete a task using resources.	Teacher solicits information/ideas about what resources are available to support student work for the assigned task.	Teacher comes to specialist with an idea for a research task or with a topic and works with the specialist to further develop the idea.
Execution of Instruction	Teacher supervises student work in the library media center. Specialist provides class with a basic orientation of available resources (if appropriate) and may have made a list of relevant resources if given enough lead time. Teacher and students ask for assistance from the specialist as questions/problems arise.	Teacher and specialist provide support to students during the completion of the task: teacher primarily on the task parameters and grading expectations, specialist primarily on how to access/use resources.	Teacher and specialist each provide support to students during the completion of all aspects of the task: orienting them to the resources at hand; supporting their use of the resources and their efforts to collect, analyze, and synthesize information; and the clarification of task parameters/grading expectations.
Evaluation of Student Work	Teacher evaluates student work. Task parameters and grading expectations may or may not have been shared with the specialist in advance.	Teacher evaluates student work (the grading expectations were shared with the specialist prior to the students work in the library media center).	Teacher and specialist score student work together using a common rubric that includes criteria both within the teacher's content area and information literacy.
Reflection and Next Steps	Specialist waits to find out how it went—receives anecdotal information from teacher and/or student(s) but does not see student work or analysis of student achievement.	Teacher shares information with specialist on how it went. May submit a sample of student work or a copy of the task for the specialist's binder. Next steps are reserved until the teacher has another task in mind that requires the specialist's support.	Based on student achievement of the task, teacher and specialist draw conclusions about what the next task(s) should focus on to meet academic expectations both within teacher's content area and information literacy.

analysis, and reflection on student achievement data as a primary part of their work.

Devoting more time to assessment of student achievement requires spending less time on other tasks. The question is how much priority is given to the analysis of student work by both the library media specialist and the school in general? There is a growing body of research that a powerful library program positively impacts student achievement scores as much as 10-20% (Loertscher and Lance 2003). To realize such gains, however, the focus of the specialist must be broader than merely daily operations. That focus requires more personnel assistance, both in the form of volunteers and paid assistants, however, it is much more cost effective to have the most expensive employee(s) in the library media center focused on the most important priorities of the learning environment.

When teachers bring their students in as an "isolated event" (Figure 2), library media specialists can still evaluate student performance on information and technology literacy standards with or without involvement of the classroom teacher. The challenge is to have a way of evaluating students that is highly efficient (because of a minimal amount of time to supervise many different students with whom there are differing degrees of familiarity). One of the most promising practices for this is to track student work into a basic database using a handheld device (i.e., Palm). Imagine a basic database that has the names of all of the students in the school (this can interface with existing school software) and the information literacy standards for each grade level(s). A basic rating system such as Novice

Learner, Apprentice Learner, or InfoStar (2004) by Koelichn and Zwaan could be adopted so that library media specialists could evaluate student performance with or without collaboration from the supervising teacher. This would provide critical data about the overall proficiency of students to use as leverage for more time and broader access to students for improvement of student achievement. It also would reveal which students have greater opportunities to learn because of the frequency and quality of their access to the library media center.

When teachers and library media specialists work as part of a "coordinated effort" (Figure 2), specialists can advocate including a strong information literacy component to classroom assessments and rubrics either designed on behalf of or in conjunction with the individual teacher. This should be a natural pairing because information literacy is embedded in virtually all subject area content standards and requires limited additional effort/planning time on the part of the classroom teacher. Not only can specialists coordinate with teachers on this one-on-one basis, but also at the department/content level by applying the same approach to the development or refinement of core assessments (i.e., research requirement, I-search project, family tree visual, WebQuest). By analyzing existing tasks and student work samples, specialists can propose revisions to the task and scoring criteria so that the focus is sharpened on targeted information and technology literacy skills in addition to department/grade level expectations.

When teachers and library media specialists work in "partnership"

(Figure 2), there is a powerful opportunity to ensure that the tasks require students to demonstrate their competency in the subject. "The goal of competency makes clear that the aim of education is not the ability to acquire and retain information—the traditional formulation… [it is the] ability to do something with what you know—to apply information in the search for a solution to a problem or to create new knowledge—creates an expectation of more rigorous forms of accountability and assessment"(Wagner 1997, 45). This partnership involves teacher and specialist working together in the design, delivery, and evaluation of student learning. While this is the most time consuming of all three forms of collaboration, it does maximize the effectiveness of the instruction and can have the most significant impact on student achievement.

To some, this article may be an untenable proposal; to others, it is a call to action; and to still others, it is a confirmation of what they have been saying all along. Regardless of individual perspectives on this issue, the fact is that without the authority to work with students in a rigorous, relevant, and consistent manner, no curriculum document on the national, state, or local levels will ever impact student learning.

Resources

Koechlin, Carol, and Sandi Zwann. *Build Your Own Information Literate School.* Hi Willow Research and Publishing, 2003.

Loertscher, David V., and Keith Lance. *Powering Achievement: School Library Media Programs Make a Difference: The Evidence.* 2nd ed. Hi Willow, 2002.

Wagner, Tony. *Making the Grade: Reinvesting in America's Schools.* Routledgefalmer, 1997. ✋

~·USE THIS PAGE!·~

Student Learning in the Library Media Center
What am I here for? What are my students here for?

Basic Task Description	Individual/Teacher Expectations	Areas of Information Literacy (check those that apply)
		☐ Define and clarify ☐ Locate and retrieve ☐ Select, process, and record data ☐ Analyze ☐ Synthesize ☐ Share and use ☐ Reflection

What areas of Information Literacy are new for you/your students?

What areas do you/your students have experience in but still may have questions about?

What areas do you/your students have a lot of experience and success in?

For more information about this page, see the article "Where Does Your Authority Come From?: Empowering the Library Media Specialist as a True Partner in Student Achievement" by Allison Zmuda (*SLMAM*, September 2006, pages 19-22).

structor who knows information sources in order to build collections that match learning needs while supporting deep learning; she or he can serve as a learning specialist. School librarians as learning specialists can offer leadership that ensures students have opportunities to experience learning that is meaningful. Through this role, the school librarian can work to gather necessary data that shows learner-based results of instructional practice.

To create a successful student- and learning-centered school library, solutions for addressing instructional practice and program planning, as well as assessment strategies, should be combined into a holistic approach to program improvement. This work should be posed to answer questions such as: Is this worth doing? Does this cause student learning? How do we know? With this type of leadership, any advocacy effort will be strengthened with data and evidence that place student learning at the heart of school libraries, showing that school librarians are teachers and learning specialists and that library programs are an invaluable and necessary part of every school.

References

American Association of School Librarians. *Empowering Learners: Guidelines for School Library Media Programs.* Chicago, Ill.: American Library Association, 2009.

Anderson, P. H. *Planning School Library Media Facilities.* Hamden, Conn.: Library Professional Publications, 1990.

Callison, Daniel. "Effective Instruction Based on Evidence-Based Strategies." *School Library Media Activities Monthly* 23, no. 8 (April 2007): 45–47.

Donham, Jean. "Assignments Worth Doing." *School Library Monthly* 28, no. 2 (November 2011): 5–7.

Hamilton, Buffy. "Getting There Together: Assessing Student Learning." Presentation for the New Jersey Library Cooperative, February 2011. http://tiny.cc/rkb56 (accessed January 4, 2012).

Harada, Violet H., and Joan M. Yoshina. *Assessing for Learning: Librarians and Teachers as Partners.* 2nd ed., rev. Santa Barbara, Calif.: Libraries Unlimited, 2010.

Harada, Violet H., and Joan M. Yoshina. "Assessing Learning: The Missing Piece in Instruction?" *School Library Media Activities Monthly* 22, no. 7 (March 2006): 20–23.

Kachel, Debra E. "Beyond the Library Door: The Story of Pennsylvania's HR 987." *School Library Monthly* 27, no. 7 (April 2011): 49–51.

Kuhlthau, Carol, Leslie Maniotes, and Ann K. Caspari. *Guided Inquiry: Learning in the 21st Century.* Westport, Conn.: Libraries Unlimited, 2007.

Pappas, Marjorie L. "Designing Learning for Evidence-Based Practice." *School Library Monthly* 24, no. 5 (January 2008): 20–23.

Pappas, Marjorie L. "Tools for Assessment of Learning." *School Library Media Activities Monthly* 23, no. 9 (May 2007): 21–25.

Stripling, Barbara. "Inquiry: Inquiring Minds Want to Know." *School Library Media Activities Monthly* 25, no. 1 (September 2008): 50–52.

Tilley, Carol. "The True Value of the Work We Do." *School Library Monthly* 27, no. 8 (May/June 2011): 45–47.

Todd, Ross. "Charting Student Learning." *School Library Monthly* 28, no. 3 (December 2011): 5–8.

"Use This Page: Assessing the Research Process." *School Library Monthly* 26, no. 4 (December 2009): 2.

"Use This Page: Assessment Tool: Levels of Communication, Cooperation, and Collaboration with Teachers." *School Library Media Activities Monthly* 23, no. 2 (October 2006): 2.

"Use This Page: Designing Learning for Evidence-Based Practice." *School Library Media Activities Monthly* 23, no. 2 (January 2008): 2.

"Use This Page: Inquiry-based Teaching and Learning-The Role of the Library Media Specialist." *School Library Media Activities Monthly* 25, no. 1 (September 2008): 2.

"Use This Page: Planning and Assessing Inquiry-based Learning" *School Library Monthly* 26, no. 1 (September 2009): 2.

"Use This Page: Steps to Designing Inquiry-Based Units." *School Library Media Activities Monthly* 25, no. 3 (November 2008): 2.

"Use This Page: Student Learning in the Library Media Center: What am I here for? What are my students here for?" *School Library Media Activities Monthly* 23, no. 1 (September 2006): 2.

"Use This Page: Taking Action: Saving School Libraries." *School Library Monthly* 27, no. 5 (February 2011): 2.

Zmuda, Allison. "The End of an Era . . . Falling Off a Cliff." *School Library Monthly* 27, no. 1 (September/October 2010): 5–7.

Zmuda, Allison. "Six Steps to Saving Your School Library Program." *School Library Media Activities Monthly* 27, no. 5 (February 2011): 45–48.

Zmuda, Allison. "Where Does Your Authority Come From? Empowering the Library Media Specialist as a True Partner in Student Achievement." *School Library Media Activities Monthly* 23, no. 1 (September 2006): 19–22.

Zmuda, Allison, and Violet H. Harada. *Librarians as a Learning Specialists: Meeting the Imperative for the 21st Century.* Westport, Conn.: Libraries Unlimited, 2008a.

Zmuda, Allison, and Violet H. Harada. "Reframing the Library Media Specialist as a Learning Specialist." *School Library Media Activities Monthly* 24, no. 8 (April 2008b): 42–47.

Additional Resources

Buerkett, Rebecca. "Inquiry and Assessment Using Web 2.0 Tools." *School Library Monthly* 28, no. 1 (September/October 2011): 21–24.

Donham, Jean. "Deep Learning through Concept-based Inquiry." *School Library Monthly* 27, no. 1 (September/October 2010): 8–11.

Donham, Jean. *Enhancing Teaching and Learning: A Leadership Guide for School Library Media Specialists.* New York: Neal Schuman, 2008.

Duvall, Sara, Kristal Jaaskelainen, and Peter Pasque. "Grassroots Google Tools: ePortfolio in Assessment and Curriculum Integration." *School Library Monthly* 27, no. 7 (April 2011): 23–25.

Fontichiaro, Kristin. *21st-Century Learning in School Libraries.* Santa Barbara, Calif.: Libraries Unlimited, 2009.

Fontichiaro, Kristin (compiler). "Nudging toward Inquiry: Formative Assessment." *School Library Monthly* 27, no.6 (March 2011): 11–12.

Fontichiaro, Kristin (compiler). "Nudging toward Inquiry: Formative Assessment: Using Feedback." *School Library Monthly* 28, no. 7 (April 2012): 51–52.

Fontichiaro, Kristin (compiler). "Nudging toward Inquiry: Summative Assessment." *School Library Monthly* 27, no. 7 (April 2011): 12–13.

Fontichiaro, Kristin (compiler). "Nudging toward Inquiry: Summative Assessment." *School Library Monthly* 28, no. 8 (May/June 2012): 48–49.

Fredrick. Kathy. "Assessment for Program Growth." *School Library Monthly* 28, no. 3 (December 2011): 23–25.

Harada, Violet H. "Building Evidence Folders for Learning through Library Media Centers." *School Library Media Activities Monthly* 23, no. 3 (November 2006): 25–30.

Harada, Violet H. "From Eyeballing to Evidence: Assessing for Learning in Hawaii Library Media Centers." *School Library Media Activities Monthly* 24, no. 3 (November 2007): 21–25.

Harada, Violet H. "Self-Assessment: Challenging Students to Take Charge of Learning." *School Library Monthly* 26, no. 10 (June 2010): 13–15.

Logan, Debra Kay. "Being Heard . . . Advocacy + Evidence + Students = Impact!" *School Library Media Activities Monthly* 23, no. 1 (September 2006): 46–48.

Pappas, Marjorie L. "Reflection as Self-Assessment." *School Library Monthly* 27, no. 3 (December 2010): 5–8.

Preddy, Leslie B. "Research Reflections, Journaling, and Exit Slip." *School Library Media Activities Monthly* 25, no. 2 (October 2008): 22–23.

Preddy, Leslie B. "Student Inquiry in the Research Process, Part 5: Inquiry Research Conclusion & Reflection." *School Library Media Activities Monthly* 23, no. 7 (March 2003): 24–27, 51.

Purcell, Melissa. "Digital Portfolios: A Valuable Teaching Tool." *School Library Monthly* 27, no. 6 (March 2011): 21–22.

Purcell, Melissa. "Use This Page: Digital Portfolio Assessment." *School Library Monthly* 27, no. 6 (March 2011): 2.

Wallace, Virginia, and Whitney Norwood Husid. *Collaborating for Inquiry-Based Learning: School Librarians and Teachers Partner for Student Achievement.* Santa Barbara, Calif.: Libraries Unlimited, 2011.

Zmuda, Allison. "Hitch Your Wagon to a Mission Statement." *School Library Media Activities Monthly* 24, no. 1 (September 2007): 24–26.

Zmuda, Allison. "Leap of Faith—Take the Plunge into a 21st-Centry Conception of Learning." *School Library Monthly* 26, no. 3 (November 2009): 16–18.

Zmuda, Allison. "What Does It Really Look Like When Students Are Learning in the Library Media Center?" *School Library Media Activities Monthly* 25, no. 1 (September 2008): 25–27.

3

Taking a Proactive Stance: Advocacy to Activism

Ann M. Martin

Sometimes luck happens. A winning lottery ticket is purchased. A phenomenal basketball shot rims in to win a game. The tree falls into the yard, avoiding the house. But assured success does not depend on luck. It is the result of sustained progress toward a goal. Success takes discipline, persistence, knowledge, practice, and vision. Sometimes it takes failure to know when to adjust the plan. Attaining desired goals means being prepared and knowing what strategies and processes achieve results. Following a plan minimizes risk and maximizes positive outcomes. Like training programs for high-performing athletes, successful library advocacy plans result from mapping out goals, developing objectives, implementing action steps, evaluating, reassessing, and communicating.

School librarians are facing a reduction in numbers, and school library programs are being cut right out of district budgets. It is difficult to not feel vulnerable. Whether the decreased library budget is insufficient to meet the needs of learners or whether librarians are struggling to enlist collaborative support for a library program, the reality of each situation demands action. It is tempting to point a finger identifying a person, program, or policy that is hurting the library program, yet name-blaming will neither improve nor institutionalize the library as critical and essential for students in the minds of users and decision makers. The key to survival is to proactively develop an advocacy plan that expands and changes as the educational landscape shifts, involves users and decision makers in the process, and shows them why and how the library is a valuable program. It also moves school librarians and others into activism.

Developing Leadership

Creating a proactive advocacy plan requires leadership skills. There are multiple theories and studies describing leadership qualities and skills. Essential to current research on librarian leadership are the dispositional studies of Gail Bush and Jami Biles Jones. Bush and Jones remind school librarians that just as students must develop 21st-century dispositions, librarians must also nurture and perfect those very same dispositions in themselves (Bush and Jones 2010, 4). Professional performance and success requires displaying dispositions such as confidence, self-direction, emotional resiliency, persistence, teamwork, and leadership. These are fundamental dispositions exhibited by leaders when designing any program or plan. School librarians must also exhibit these dispositions when implementing a proactive advocacy plan aimed at positioning the library program as the focal point of the school community.

As a proactive advocacy plan is developed, it is important for the school librarian to identify and self-assess her or his own dispositions. Analyzing weaknesses in dispositions moves these behaviors from the conceptual domain to a more concrete understanding. If a school librarian lacks confidence, then she or he must determine what is underlying the timid, unsure feelings. If self-direction is weak, then the school librarian must determine what research would be helpful or identify who can provide assistance to move forward. Through discussion with others and self-reflections, the school librarian can begin to clarify the vision necessary to create an advocacy plan. The school librarian must identify reactions to barriers that arise: Is the instinct to give up or explore other means and determine how to maneuver around obstacles? When a person starts to waver, who or what will help strengthen resolve? If antagonism is feared, who can be identified to join the team and prompt cooperation? If the drive needed to get a plan off the ground is lacking, what procedures can be put into action that will guide the process? Awareness of dispositions and consciously assessing related strengths and weaknesses helps to improve leadership behaviors.

Leaders take deliberate actions and use documentation to substantiate how the librarian and library program contribute to school success and student learning. A leader strengthens ties to the community starting with the students and school staff and then extending those ties to the wider community. By delegating, collaborating, and negotiating, leaders consistently and systematically nurture an inquiry-based, interactive learning environment. Successful leaders achieve this by knowing user needs, understanding school and district initiatives, and then working relentlessly to connect library instruction and programs to each. Reaching out to users and providing opportunities to address student and staff concerns trigger increased awareness of library resources and demand for the library program. Potential advocates are developed as members of the learning community and the greater community participate in positive library experiences. A long-term advocacy plan begins when leaders who understand the vision for the library program create a broad network of users-turned-advocates who are available to speak to decision makers in times of need, becoming activists.

Leaders examine their individual dispositions, meet user needs, and extend the program to the wider community to create a network of advocates. This chapter provides processes to guide leadership of a succinct, organized, goal-oriented advocacy plan. It explains how leaders review the changing landscape of education and analyze how school libraries are essential to this environment. Leaders understand that schools are bureaucracies where resources are limited. They know that when one department receives more dollars, time, or resources, then another part of the organization often suffers a loss. For an advocacy plan to be successful, leaders analyze decisions, challenge barriers, and alter goals. Leaders create advocates each time they put systems in place that result in consistent, improved access to supporters.

Building Advocates

Broad-based support begins within the school. A beginning step is to seek information that will strengthen the value of the library within the school. For example, it is important to identify what is significant to each department, grade level, and staff member. One way librarians do this is by developing and administering a survey. The survey functions as a needs analysis as well as an assessment tool to confirm whether the library program is addressing these user concerns. Since powerful information is contained in the survey results, it is important that the librarian review the data before anyone else. Reflection enables the librarian to approach challenges identified from the survey with confidence.

Once the data are compiled, the librarian constructs a team of users from within the school building. This team includes students who represent diverse cultures and learning styles as well as teachers from a variety of curriculum areas. As the team reviews the results of the survey, team members assist by brainstorming and developing solutions to user needs (Martin 2012). It is the responsibility of the librarian, as leader of the library program, to guide the team to resolutions that support library best practices. Providing the team with documents based on national library program guidelines and standards that link to the American Association of School Librarians' *Empowering Learners* (2009) and *Standards for the 21st-Century Learner* (2007) informs the team and provides background information that helps them place survey data in the proper context. This information also instills confidence in the team. As issues are discussed, the team appreciates recommendations from the librarian on how the library program can solve their individual curriculum resource needs. At the same time, the librarian is provided with a better sense of user needs and the unique needs of individual curriculum departments through team members' input. As a result of this work, the team members will act as advocates when the library program is requesting specific resources or launching initiatives discussed and researched by the group.

Every person in the community has the potential to be a library champion. This concept is important to building broad-based advocates as essential to a long-term advocacy plan. Numbers do make a difference when convincing decision makers. For this reason, it is necessary to identify individuals within and beyond the walls of the school to support the library program. Determining who the target audiences are and how to identify and elicit their support is the first step in a long-term advocacy plan. Librarians are often so intent on drawing support from direct users of the library program that they find themselves too busy to extend out into the community. Although it is imperative to meet issues at the building level, when it comes to advocacy it is important to extend conscious outreach to the wider community. Successful advocacy plans are founded on the premise that all segments of the community are vital components to developing preemptive grassroots efforts.

Every library experience provides an opportunity to introduce the library to a segment of the community. One example of this is when a high school librarian found that alumnae of the school were a natural group to invite to events. A new school opened and was named for a high school that had been closed many years earlier. The alumnae of the original high school were more than excited to be a part of the new school. This librarian created a special section in the library dedicated to the history of the school and its alumnae. As a result of her outreach, graduates from the original high school were considered very important people at events and activities. This librarian brought recognition to the library program by constructing a bridge between the old school and the new school. The richness of each new experience continues to foster positive supporters from a group of benefactors who live in the community and are connected to businesses and volunteer organizations.

Another way to extend support to the wider community is by connecting initiatives to as many individuals and groups as possible. A librarian who develops discerning vision realizes connections between the library, all instructional lessons, and the community. Extending the connections even further, the librarian capitalizes by establishing links from the library to every school project and event. An effective way to do this is by organizing a list of community resources that are potential materials for library lessons and school projects. For example, if a class comes to the library to research the environmental impact of coal mining, the librarian can determine if there are experts in the community on environmental issues, coal mining, or manufacturing issues related to the lesson. Contacting these experts and involving them in the lesson either in face-to-face or digital format enriches the project for the students and informs community members of student interests. Issuing an invitation to these partners so they can view online or in person the final student work validates the community member's contribution. In addition, it provides community partners with information to share with their business colleagues and makes learning connections to the library.

Librarians realize that parents like to know when their student has projects on display in the library or if they achieve positive recognition in the library. But as students continue through school from elementary to secondary levels, it is more difficult to involve parents. Inviting parents to events is an effective outreach technique. Even if the parents are unable to come to the school, the invitation informs them about their student's accomplishments and creates concrete connections between the library program and academic success. Other outreach may naturally result from displaying student work on the library Web page and sending parents an e-mail with a hyperlink to the page.

Building advocates evolves naturally when librarians connect library instruction and initiatives to the school community and the local community. To do this, the librarian starts by identifying decision makers and local groups as potential outreach opportunities and analyzes their interests, needs, and agendas. In this way, a wide network of potential advocates can be informed of relevant events through open invitations and publicity. This involves consciously mapping out who should be notified and included in specific events and why. As a result, strategic partnerships can be encouraged and developed by linking library initiatives to particular people or groups based on their interests and needs.

This type of advocacy can be exemplified in the following example. A school library initiative sponsored a "One-Community One-Book" program. For example, Garth Stein's book *The Art of Racing in the Rain* was selected for a One-Community One-Book program for the students and community to read. Part of the outreach included making connections to local animal shelters and the community NASCAR raceway complex. The extension of this library-based program was far reaching; it enriched student experiences, promoted reading, provided meaningful discussions, and involved the community. Advocates emerged from these connections as local businesses owners understood the importance of the school library and saw links to their business interests and needs. Developing community connections is a starting point when building a proactive advocacy plan and becomes easier to identify with practice.

Analyzing Organizations

Before the librarian actually formulates a written advocacy plan, it is essential to recognize that behaviors in the school will positively or negatively affect each goal, objective, and action step. These behaviors spring from how decisions are determined in the school. Some might question how analysis of administrator and colleague decision-making is important to being proactive. In reality it has everything to do with successfully positioning agendas so that the school community and its leadership will accept and support ideas and projects. Advocates are created each time initiatives are pushed through the system. On the other hand, enemies can be made if the librarian neglects to understand the reactions of colleagues to new ideas. Knowing what is important to decision makers and colleagues and providing positive experiences associated with the library are important to building an advocacy plan. To do this, librarians need to understand the decision-making process in their school. Specifically, they need an awareness of their administrators' leadership styles because it will dictate how to best position the advocacy plan.

Observing and documenting the way challenges and issues are solved in an organization assists in understanding what influences the actions of decision makers. Lee Bolman and Terrence Deal developed a practical method to examine leadership. Their work emphasizes that multiple factors are working side by side in any organization, affecting management decisions and consequently program outcomes. According to Bolman and Deal, the dominant behaviors exhibited by leaders ultimately direct how the organization runs. Bolman and Deal summarized leadership into four views or frames: structural, human resource, political, and symbolic (Bolman and Deal 2008). Analyzing school leadership through these four frames provides clear evidence of what is fundamental in order to successfully move library agendas through the decision-making process. Librarians who take time to analyze the organization will find greater success in getting needs met for the library program while developing administrators and others as supporters, moving them to actively speak for the importance of the school library.

When considering which frames are predominant in a school, there are key indicators that assist in determining leadership preference in a school. Bolman and Deal (2008) point out the following about each frame. A leader who creates clear goals, rules, policies, and a specific chain of command works in the *structural frame*. A leader who is guided by the *political frame* will advocate, negotiate, and value partnerships. With the *human resource frame*, leaders invest in people and typically empower workers and facilitate change rather than mandate decisions. Leaders who favor the *symbolic frame* develop the school culture to provide a sense of shared goals; they do this through metaphors, graphics, and slogans. Each of these views is inherent in every school environment. The librarian who analyzes the organization to determine how leaders and colleagues in the school will react to library program requests has a better opportunity to achieve needed program changes.

For a librarian to successfully implement an advocacy plan, there needs to be a full understanding of what activities, events, and actions will be accepted or rejected by the organization. Filtering each through the four frames provides the librarian with important information to consider during initiation and implementation of the plan.

Here is how this works. Consider that an objective in the advocacy plan states, "Visibility for the library program will increase by expanding use through access to online resources." Begin with the structural frame to determine what processes need to be followed to ensure technology infrastructure will support increased online demand. This includes filling out proper forms and following the technology department's established chain of command.

Next consider the human resource frame and list what human resource needs must be met for this to be successful. Find answers to such questions as: Is there manpower available to design the launching point for digital resources? Will users need training? How much time will the librarian invest to launch the initiative? Investigating these issues will increase the acceptance of the initiative by people in the organization because their needs are identified and explored.

At this point, determine if political issues will arise when the plan is introduced. Find answers to such questions as: Are there colleagues who will sense loss if time, money, and resources are directed toward implementation of digital access to library materials? What curriculum departments will benefit from digital resources? Which colleagues will most probably collaborate to select resources targeting their content areas? Based on answers to these questions, develop a list of probable supporters for implementation of digital access to resources. Also, identify possible adversaries. A proactive stance minimizes opposition by managing information. This information is directed toward answering questions and dealing with concerns of advocates and adversaries. Being proactive often enables librarians to achieve possible solutions before anticipated resistance emerges.

Use the symbolic frame to determine how marketing can improve the success of the initiative. Is there a branding for the digital resources that will provide users with a sense of identity? Will this branding incorporate school and library symbols? Decide what logos, metaphors, and slogans will be accepted. By examining this advocacy goal in a systematic manner, the project has a greater chance of success.

Librarians who analyze the organization so that processes, people, politics, and marketing related to an initiative are evaluated are thinking ahead. They are proactive because they are taking actions and anticipating organizational issues in advance of implementing the goal.

Creating Plans

Often a discouraging event will precipitate action. Outrage motivates the public to speak up when the power goes out right before the Super Bowl game. Librarians become outraged when decision makers misunderstand the importance of the library program. Unfortunately, librarians cannot create the same momentum that disappointed Super Bowl fans can initiate. Creating an overnight plan of action when a crisis arises is daunting and unrealistic. The reality is that a deeply embedded understanding for and belief in the need for school libraries begins with a long-term focus on building user and community ownership. First and foremost is the need to create a relevant instructional program that meets the needs of students and staff to widen the vibrancy of the library program and to increase users. An extension of this effort is to make connections to the greater community to establish an understanding of the school library programs and its value outside the walls of the school. Through successful outreach, advocates will emerge to address decision makers as the need arises. An advocacy plan is a deliberate attempt to engage supportive voices within and outside the walls of the library in order to deliver a specific message to decision makers. These voices convey a consistent, succinct message over time. Crafting a unified message is not a chance happening but emanates from a focused, laser-like action plan based on specific goals, objectives, and action steps. Advocacy plans are fluid documents that address immediate and future needs of the library program and adapt to changing circumstances in and outside the school.

An effective action plan must be based on the vision and goals established for the library program. Clearly defined vision statements are powerful tools that provide the library staff and the school with a picture of the future of the library program (Martin 2012, chapter 3). An example of a school library vision statement is: *The library program led by a certified school librarian serves as the intellectual and social center of the school, promoting academic and lifelong learning.* An advocacy statement developed from this shared vision might be: *Student academic success and lifelong learning are dependent on philosophical and financial support for access to school libraries led by certified school librarians.* Anchoring the advocacy statement in the shared library vision creates a foundation for the action plan. The advocacy plan should be developed to support the advocacy statement and describe desired outcomes, have measurable stated objectives, and provide specific action steps for implementation. There may be several goals, many objectives, and dozens of action steps. Each element is important to move the advocacy plan forward; each will address a specific need that should improve the library program and develop advocates.

Developing a long-term advocacy plan is attainable once a clear message is created and the end results are defined. As with the vision statement, formalizing an advocacy plan is most effective when constituents contribute, so the next step is to involve the library team when defining and implementing library initiatives. Using the advocacy statement *Student academic success and lifelong learning are dependent on philosophical and financial support for access to school libraries led by certified school librarians,* the team brainstorms potential solutions. They identify and confront one issue at a time in order to provide focused creative thinking toward each key phrase in the advocacy statement. At this point, distinct lists of concerns and ideas form the backbone of an advocacy plan.

For example, a sample goal may be to increase access to the library. The effect of increased access will be realized through more users who will have greater satisfaction and develop a regular need for use of the library program. As changes emerge in the landscape of technology, user needs also change, which creates opportunities for additional access points to library resources. A specific action step for this sample goal could be to create an application (app) for students to access digital resources from smart phones. The objective related to the goal may be: to increase use of library by 25 percent through use of the app, to be implemented at the beginning of the school year. The next step is for the library team to filter this action step through the four frames. The four-frames analysis will address concerns or issues that surface. By reviewing each stated objective and specific action step, the advocacy plan becomes a map that provides measurable steps to improve activism.

Another element of the team's work is to identify varied avenues for circulating a succinct branding message to users, decision makers, and the community. The team should explore and list the people, policies, practices, and environmental issues that may be hindering philosophical and financial support of the library program. Also, team members should compile a list of various methods that can be used to deliver the advocacy statement to the community.

An advocacy plan needs to be adaptable and evaluated periodically to ensure that identified issues are still relevant. Reviewing what is working with the plan and what is not provides opportunities to improve and change the plan over time. Altering the plan to reflect what is important in the current environment allows for it to remain relevant. The benefit of relevancy is that user satisfaction and activism will be continuous. As a result, outrage does not need to drive librarian action because advocates will emerge and communicate the value of the library program and the librarian when interacting with decision makers.

Overcoming Barriers

Once the advocacy plan is developed and filtered through the four frames, chances of success are good. But what if negative issues arise? Is the reaction to give up or to realize there are other resources available? Emotional resiliency is a disposition needed when disappointments arise. This is the ability to remain flexible and innovative when outcomes take unexpected turns. Emotional resiliency helps librarians deal with setbacks to implementation of an advocacy plan and gain the understanding that adversity is not a personal attack. Emotional resiliency is strengthened each time a difficulty is overcome and progress is made toward a goal. As each obstacle is resolved, confidence and determination are reinforced and librarians discover there are multiple ways to overcome barriers.

Understanding why barriers arise is important. Often it is the result of miscommunication, fear, or misunderstanding of how a goal or objective benefits a person or the school (Martin 2012, chapter 5). This type of analysis de-emphasizes opposition as personal and is a reminder that the plan was developed by a team of stakeholders. The plan and the problems associated with it are owned by the team that created it. Therefore, it is important to focus on linking the cause of resistance to an idea or effort and to avoid targeting a person. Instead, the goal should be to determine what is generating a reaction from that person. Often a process is broken, resulting in miscommunication or misunderstanding. In the educational environment, scarce resources create fear. Determine the root cause of fear that is producing resistance to the plan. When addressing opposition, librarians need to remember that fixing a process is more quickly attainable than trying to change a person. Since each action step was filtered through the four frames, it is best to go back to notes related to that particular action step. The notes may identify reasons for the negative reaction and assist with understanding why resistance is occurring.

There are tools available that help determine the cause and effect of problems, making it easier to suggest a solution. One tool is the fishbone or Ishikawa diagram, named after Kaoru Ishikawa. The importance of the fishbone diagram is that it provides visual understanding for what is preventing acceptance

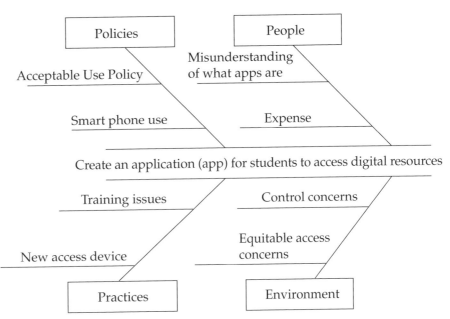

Fig. 3.1.   A visual representation of reasons for resistance to a digital resource application (app).

of an action item. The Ishikawa diagram is also called a *cause-and-effect diagram* because the indicators growing out of the spine of the fish are used to list the potential causes of the problem (Shashkin and Kiser 1993, 173). The diagram looks somewhat like a fishbone, with the problem identified in the center.

Figure 3.1 is a fishbone diagram that explores the problems arising from the action step intended to create an application (app) for students to access digital resources from smart phones. Referring to the fishbone diagram, note the challenges identified when a librarian decided to implement a digital resource application. The diagram shows the librarian and library team that certain policies must be revised, some practices need to be updated, colleagues' fears need to be understood and calmed, and concerns related to the educational environment must be addressed. In order to dissolve the barriers, the team develops solutions to counter each issue identified in the fishbone diagram.

Successful librarians develop emotional resiliency when they use processes to examine and solve negative issues. These processes create positive energy around resistance to the advocacy plan. They place the focus on problem solving instead of blaming individuals, and provide a constructive means to investigate the causes of opposition and acknowledge ways to further the plan. Most of all, they enable the librarian to view barriers as opportunities for improved communication of the advocacy plan while fostering emotional resiliency.

Measuring Success

A proactive advocacy plan is like an insurance policy; payment is made into the plan with the hope it will never be used. At the same time, the investment pays off if an occasion arises when extra help is needed. Success is measured by never having to go on the defensive, never having to argue for the library, and never having to enter into a debate to save the librarian position. The proactive advocacy plan means that decision makers view the library program as positively vital for students and continue to support it, even in tough times.

Instituting a long-term advocacy plan with action steps provides opportunities to build data. Data silence negative proposals to cut or eliminate the library program. As action plans are put in motion, it is important to collect data before each new initiative is implemented. It is just as essential to continue to accumulate data as the plan evolves, benchmarking progress to illustrate marked viability and demand for the library program and the librarian as an instructional leader. Data are unemotional, measure success, and establish a case. (See the appendix, page 106, for "Use This Page: Data-Driven Program Development: A Quick Guide.") In the action step example where an application was created for students to access digital resources, data collected prior to its implementation showed that in-school use of the databases was much greater than home access. The first month after implementation of the application, statistics indicated a 20 percent increased use of online access. At the end of several months, out-of-school usage rose 30 percent. Each action step in the advocacy plan provides opportunities to collect data.

Data serve as an evaluative tool to make adjustments to the advocacy plan. Should collected data indicate that progress is not being achieved at the rate expected, then analysis of that aspect of the plan is necessary. Using the fishbone diagram, the action step can be reviewed to determine what is contributing to negative data. Once again the team needs to determine if the action step is being hindered because of policies, people, practices, or environmental issues. Solutions to counter negative effects need to be brainstormed, and revisions to the plan must occur. Data keep the advocacy plan relevant to current needs in the educational environment.

Being proactive means continually staying ahead of the issues and being forward thinking. It means scanning the educational environment and anticipating user, administrator, and district needs. Periodic checks on progress of the plan and noting accomplishments are critical to staying current. Data also serve as a communication tool for informing users, stakeholders, decision makers, and community members. It is important to continually advertise data verifying the contribution of the library program, embedding value, and showing the need for the program in relationship to students and learning, teachers and teaching. Build on the momentum from each positive piece of data. Let decision makers know their support is paying off. As funding and philosophical support builds, decision makers become intrinsically motivated to keep the library program strong. This is the best type of advocacy.

Setting a proactive advocacy plan in motion takes time and effort. Its effectiveness accumulates over months and years. Voices of supporters are developed as the plan becomes deeply rooted in the library and educational agenda. With a common message and branding, advocates have the tools they need to speak up when necessary. The message can appear on flyers, bookmarks, instructional materials, and Web sites. It may be a great tagline in speeches. The message can be used by the principal at Parent Teacher Association (PTA) meetings, district meetings, or school board meetings. The more the message is heard, the more it will be internalized.

In Summary

Whether the decreased library budget is insufficient to meet the needs of learners or whether librarians are struggling to enlist collaborative support for a library program, the reality of these issues demands action. A proactive advocacy plan strengthens ties to the community while creating a broad network of users-turned-advocates who become available to speak to decision makers in times of need. Whether these advocates are internal or external to the school, their voices and support benefit the library program.

Essential elements such as developing leadership dispositions, building advocates, analyzing organizational behaviors, creating plans, and overcoming barriers form the basis for creating a successful plan. A librarian who exhibits leadership by delegating, collaborating, and negotiating will provide consistent and systematic nurturing of an effective advocacy plan. It is through connecting library initiatives relevant to the extended community that advocates emerge because community ownership for each goal, objective, and action step results.

Librarians must understand that multiple factors are working side by side in any organization, affecting decisions and consequently outcomes. Analyzing the school leadership through the structural, human resource, political, and symbolic frames developed by Lee Bolman and Terrance Deal provides clear evidence of what is fundamental to successfully move library agendas through the decision-making process. An effective action plan is based on the vision and goals of the advocacy message developed by a team of contributors. The plan describes the desired outcomes, has measurable stated objectives, and provides specific action steps for implementation.

Sometimes setbacks occur during implementation of the advocacy plan. There are tools available to assist in determining the cause and effect of problems. Using a deliberate process approach is a constructive means to investigate causes of opposition and to acknowledge ways to further the plan. Periodic checks on the progress of the plan and noting accomplishments are critical to staying current. Gathering, analyzing, interpreting, and sharing data related to goals are essential to garnering support for the library program. Using data to recognize success or to realize needed adjustments to the plan contributes to attaining goals and keeps the advocacy plan current and on target.

So how is success confirmed? Obviously, the greatest measure of success is when the message is heard from advocates, when they voice opinions that show they believe in the value of the librarian and the library program. Then it can be known that library advocacy has come full circle.

References

Bolman, Lee, and Terry Deal. *Reframing Organizations: Artistry, Choice, and Leadership*, Kindle ed. San Francisco: Jossey-Bass, 2008.

Bolman, Lee, and Terry Deal. *Reframing Organizations: The Leadership Kaleidoscope*. n.d. http://www.tnellen.com/ted/tc/bolman.html (accessed October 10, 2011).

Bush, Gail, and Jami Biles Jones. *Tales Out of the School Library: Developing Professional Dispositions*. Santa Barbara, Calif.: Libraries Unlimited, 2010.

Martin, Ann M. *Seven Steps to an Award-Winning School Library Program*. 2nd ed. Santa Barbara, Calif.: Libraries Unlimited, 2012.

Shashkin, Marshall, and Kenneth J. Kiser. *Putting Total Quality Management to Work: What TQM Means, How to Use It and How to Sustain It over the Long Run.* San Francisco: Berrett-Koehler Publishers, 1993.

"Use This Page: Data-Driven Program Development: A Quick Guide." *School Library Monthly* 28, no. 2 (November 2011): 2.

Additional Resources

American Association of School Librarians. *Empowering Learners: Guidelines for School Library Media Programs.* Chicago, Ill.: American Library Association, 2009.

American Association of School Librarians Standards for the 21st-Century Learner." *American Library Association.* www.ala.org/ala/mgrps/divs/aasl/guidelinesandstandards/learning standards/AASL_Learning_Standards_2007.pdf (accessed October 3, 2011).

Coatney, Sharon. "Leadership for Hard Times." *School Library Monthly* 27, no. 6 (March 2011): 38–39.

Dutton-Ewbank, Ann. "Values-Oriented Factors Leading to Retention of School Librarian Positions: A School District Case Study." *School Library Media Research* 14 (January 2011): 2.

Hand, Dorcas. "What Can Teacher-Librarians Do to Promote Their Work and the School Library Media Program? Keep Everyone in the Loop: Constant Advocacy." *Teacher Librarian* 36, no. 2 (December 2008): 26–27.

Haycock, Ken. "Leadership Is about You." *School Library Monthly* 26, no. 6 (February 2010): 42–44.

Haycock, Ken. "Leading Change." *School Library Monthly* 28, no. 4 (January 2012): 32–34.

Howard, Jodi K. "Advocacy through Relationships." *School Library Monthly* 26, no. 2 (October 2009): 44–45.

Fredrick, Kathy. "Assessment for Program Growth." *School Library Monthly* 28, no. 3 (December 2011): 23–25.

Johns, Sara Kelly. "School Librarians Taking the Leadership Challenge." *School Library Monthly* 27, no. 4 (January 2011): 37–39.

Kaaland, Christie. "Proactive Advocacy: 'Emergency Preparedness' for the School Library." *School Library Monthly* 27, no. 4 (January 2011): 49–51.

Kachel, Debra E. "Furloughed but Not Forgotten." *School Library Monthly* 28, no. 5 (February 2012): 5–7.

Martin, Ann M. "Data Driven Leadership." *School Library Monthly* 28, no. 2 (November 2011): 31–33.

Smith, Daniella. "Educating Preservice School Librarians to Lead: A Study of Self-Perceived Transformational Leadership Behaviors." *School Library Media Research* 14 (January 2011): 5.

Stephens, Wendy Steadman. "The School Librarian as Leader: Out of the Middle, into the Foreground." *Knowledge Quest* 39, no. 5 (May/June): 18–21.

"Use This Page: Act 4 School Libraries." *School Library Monthly* 27, no. 1 (September/October 2010): 2.

Zmuda, Allison. "The End of an Era . . . Falling Off a Cliff." *School Library Monthly* 27, no. 1 (September/October 2010): 5–7.

4

Developing a Culture of Advocacy

Christie Kaaland

Never doubt that a small group of thoughtful, committed citizens can change the world. Indeed, it is the only thing that ever has.

—Margaret Mead, anthropologist

The buzz around advocacy for school libraries has come about not simply as a fad but rather as a strategy for the advancement—and possibly the future survival—of school library programs and the school librarian profession. Yet at state and national conferences when presenters, skilled in advocacy techniques, offer sessions to increase awareness and offer advocacy skills, the sessions are sparsely attended. Ignoring the need for activism will not make that need disappear. For the health and survival of the profession, today's librarians need to add "Developing a Culture of Advocacy" to the skills required of the profession.

Those who have not been actively involved in advocating for their school library program or have not begun to develop such strategies often find the idea intimidating. Yet there are manageable strategies that can be used to create varied levels and types of advocacy ranging from very basic to comprehensive, detailed, district-wide plans. Librarians can employ appropriate strategies to gain support for the continued existence of a strong school library program. The first step is having an understanding concerning attitudes and basic dispositions related to advocacy and embracing them as a professional responsibility.

Developing a Culture of Advocacy: Advocacy 101

When we are doing our job well, there is evidence of learning and growth, but is the attribution for the success being given to the strong library program and leadership of the teacher-librarian? . . . People looking in from the outside do not necessarily appreciate [that] the success of the program is a result of the expertise of the teacher-librarian to lead, make connections, and share their knowledge, skills, and attitudes with the school's learning community. Thus we are compelled to go beyond doing our job well to consider how to influence the decision-makers and influencers working outside our daily sphere. (Kerr 2011)

Although the school library profession has certainly learned that advocating for school libraries brings results, there exist certain foundational skills and knowledge and, more importantly, *dispositions* or a *culture of advocacy* that every librarian must develop in order to ensure strong, well-funded, well-supported school library programs. Certain elements are prerequisites for developing a sound culture of advocacy, a culture that will gain support from patrons and others based on the value of a strong school library. Whether the goal is to work for an individual school library or work toward funding for school libraries through statewide or federal legislation or initiatives, the following elements will help build a culture of advocacy and promote activism by school librarians and others.

A Culture of Advocacy

Advocacy Must Be about Student Learning

Above all else, the *positive impact on student learning* must stand at the very core of advocating for the school library program. Every act of advocacy must cloak itself, first and foremost, in student success. It is not enough simply to believe in school libraries and their educational value. In order to be effective, school library activists must provide decision makers, from school administrators to legislators, with sound evidence of student academic achievement. This is where successful school library activism must begin.

Resources for gathering supportive evidence and data abound. Most recently, all current state studies of the impact of school libraries on multiple criteria—from instruction and access to the achievement gap and technology—have been compiled by Deb Kachel and her school library students in a recent comprehensive compilation of impact studies, "School Library Impact Studies: The Major Findings" (Kachel 2011).

In addition, books such as that by Vi Harada and Joan Yoshina (2010) provide practical and achievable strategies for teachers and school librarians to partner in assessing learning. There are also tools such as TRAILS (Tool for Real-time Assessment of Information Literacy Skills) and the toolkit, Student Learning through Inquiry Measure (SLIM), available from the Center for International Scholarship in School Libraries (CISSL) at Rutgers.

For more specific information about evidence-based practice and assessment strategies that link school library programs to student learning, see chapter 2.

Advocacy Must Be Altruistically Motivated

By its very nature, advocacy is altruistic. Librarians must take the lead in recruiting support for a strong school library program; however, most of the actual advocating should be conducted by individuals outside the immediate school library profession (e.g., teachers, parents, students, administrators, and community members). When a librarian acts alone as the advocate for the program, it is often seen as self-serving, and decision makers, from principals to legislators, question the motive of promoting a personal agenda. Conversely, when students and parents stand in support of the library program, decision makers, whose constituents are often these same students and parents, are more likely to take heed. It sends a powerful message to decision makers when library supporters such as these speak out.

For example, when library advocates in Washington state campaigned for two years with the legislature successfully allowing the inclusion of school libraries in legislation defining libraries as "basic education," they thought their task was finished. Not so. After passage of this legislation, Spokane Mom Lisa Layera-Brunkan addressed an audience of those who had worked tirelessly for passage of this legislation. Undaunted, her message was clear: "Can you really look yourself in the mirror and say only the children of the state of Washington deserve equitable access to information, resources, and technology?" This selfless agenda was at the heart of why legislators listened and responded to Lisa's campaign. Republican Representative Skip Priest claimed, "The Spokane Moms' campaign for legislation is the strongest grassroots campaign I have seen in my 30 years in politics" (Lisa Layera-Brunkan, personal interview, April 13, 2009).

Clearly, the Spokane Moms' selfless magnanimity at the heart of this legislative campaign helped convince legislators to sponsor and sign this legislation.

Advocacy Must Be Ongoing

School librarians must lead the charge of advocacy and carry their message forward. The librarian begins the campaign of championing for the school library; activists pick up the gauntlet and carry that campaign forward as the *face* and *voice* of the advocate.

Advocacy must become a way of life and a part of everything a school librarian does. Advocacy, then, becomes a foundation of sustainability for the school library program. Each day, librarians should ask themselves, "What am I doing today that will affect student learning and how can I let others know about that impact?" Embracing this framework requires librarians to consider all audiences beyond themselves and their job, while recognizing that all school library advocacy efforts are meant to support students.

Advocates Must Be Positive

The most effective advocacy campaigns begin and end with a positive message. After all, at the heart of advocacy is a request. Whether it is legislation, school district funding, or simply continuation of the program, advocates are asking for something. In the spirit of not biting "the hand that feeds you," advocates must bring something to the table. That "something" is the desire for student success and the mission of comprehensive student services. It is then nothing more than an act of sincere and warranted appreciation for the importance of the library program that garners support from a decision maker.

Advocates Must Be Vocal and Articulate

For some, this may be the most difficult charge of school library activism. But "vocal" and "articulate" do not necessarily refer to only acts of public presentations. Important here is communicating to decision makers about how school libraries affect student learning on an ongoing basis.

Program Assessment

See the appendix, pages 102 and 103, for the following resources that will help with school library program assessment with links to learning:

"Use This Page: Taking Action: Saving School Libraries; Six Steps: Saving Your Library Program," *School Library Monthly* 27, no. 5 (February 2011). This page provides a rubric, "Six Steps: Saving Your School Library Program," from the article by Allison Zmuda, in *School Library Media Activities Monthly* (February 2010, pages 45–48).

"Use This Page: Assessment Tool: Levels of Communication, Cooperation, and Collaboration with Teachers," *School Library Media Activities Monthly* 23, no. 2 (October 2006). This page provides a simple tool for recording work with classroom teachers related to learning goals to support the article by Allison Zmuda, "Where Does Your Authority Come From? Empowering the Library Media Specialist as a True Partner in Student Achievement." *School Library Media Activities Monthly* (September 2006, pages 19–22).

Also available are the following tools:

American Association of School Librarians: *A Planning Guide for Empowering Learners with School Library Program Assessment Rubric* (available from http://aasl.eb.com/planningGuideFor EmpoweringLearnersController.htm)

Colorado State Libraries: *School Library Program Competencies—Evaluation Rubric* (available from http://www.cde.state.co.us/cdelib/powerlib/download/SchoolLibraryEvalRubric.pdf)

New York State Education Department: *School Library Media Program Evaluation (SLMPE) Rubric* (available from http://www.p12.nysed.gov/technology/library/SLMPE_rubric/)

Historically, librarians have been typecast as reserved and *not* self-promoting. This lack of self-promotion has not served the profession well. Today, all advocates must promote the academic impact of a professional school librarian in an optimistically eloquent manner, armed with data.

Many hardworking school librarians may not feel comfortable presenting their contribution at a school board or local community meeting. In fact, more powerful reception occurs if spokespersons originate outside the school library profession. Yet it is the school librarian who must lead the effort and help articulate and communicate the importance of the school library as it relates to student learning. The school librarian is the source for information for the voice of other advocates.

It is important to use a variety of avenues to constantly demonstrate the important role of the librarian as well as the school library program and to communicate that information on an ongoing basis. This can be accomplished through presentations, newsletters, e-mails, one-on-one meetings, social networking, reports, surveys, and through a strong and viable school library Web site.

Advocates Must Do Homework

The more informed the advocate is prior to promoting the library program—whether formally or informally, written or staged—the higher the likelihood for successful results. Advocates need to know what and when decisions are made, who key decision makers are, and what influences each critical decision-maker. Some "homework" assignments:

- Find out when important school district budget decisions are made and be involved in that process. Presenting school library news, information, or data to the school board just prior to budget decision-making leaves board members with a recent memory of new information centered on the school library.

- Determine the politics of the school district. Decisions pertaining to particular programs, especially decisions on smaller programs such as the full-time equivalencies (FTEs) for the district's library personnel, are often made by one individual. (Do not automatically assume this person is the district library administrator.) Find out who that decision maker is, how much influence she or he *really* has, and what you can do to make that individual your strongest ally.

- Research top job applicants prior to hires. As the school district conducts a superintendent search or as new individuals begin campaigning for school board, find out their level of support and understanding of the importance of the school library program. A few strategic phone calls can provide telling results. For example, years ago a national superintendent search for Tacoma (Washington) schools resulted in a final candidate from another state. A few random phone calls to the candidate's home district's librarians proved very telling in determining the candidate's leadership style, pedagogical priorities, and, most important, level of support for libraries.

- Better yet, ask to meet for coffee with a potential school board member. This level of personal interaction may serve to inform that school board member of the changing and important role of school libraries today. Use resources like "School Library Research Summarized: A Graduate Class Project" (Kachel 2011), Scholastic's "School Libraries Work!" (2008), or the AASL Advocacy Toolkit (http://www.ala.org/ala/mgrps/divs/aasl/aaslissues/toolkits/aasl advocacy.cfm).

Advocates Must Be Well Informed

Whether presenting formally to legislators at a school board meeting or a regularly scheduled principal meeting or informally in conversation with peers and colleagues, librarians should always carry an arsenal of constantly updated data and facts noting how school libraries affect student learning. These data should include district-specific details but may also include multiple studies of national significance (see the *AASL Advocacy Toolkit*).

Such data may address the positive influences of a school library program; for example, "Our district has shown a gradual increase in job-readiness through the ACT test scores for the past three years since the school librarians began embedding the ACT college-readiness standards in the curriculum we teach." Never miss an opportunity to include "what we teach" since many people outside the school community do not realize that school librarians do teach.

Or point out changes due to decrease in library services, such as: "Have you noticed that the district's reading scores, particularly with regard to reading comprehension, have declined by _____ in direct relation to the number of students served per certificated librarian since 2003?" (Include specific data.)

Advocates Must Be Omnipresent

When the goings-on in the library are visible in a variety of formats, they will reach a greater number of the school's community members. One primary responsibility of the librarian is the promotion of his or her school library, particularly unique programs and academic successes, so that information and data can easily be provided for advocates when opportunities arise.

Advocacy Is in Constant Motion

Advocacy is a constantly moving target: Elected officials change, superintendents retire and are replaced, new superintendents bring in outside administrators whose priorities and pedagogical leanings align with their own, and newly elected school board members come with their own agendas. Thus, without vigilant advocacy, any new decision maker can negatively affect or reverse years of support librarians have built.

A cautionary tale drawn from legislative advocacy sadly exemplifies this fact. After a two-year legislative campaign, school library advocates in Washington state confidently rested on their laurels following the successful passage of SBH 2261. As inexperienced legislative activists, these advocates were unaware that passage of a bill is only *half* the battle. Appropriations (funding) follows passage of a bill. School library advocates discontinued attendance at legislative committee meetings, which resulted in a drop to last-place funding priority as funding mandates were decided. This bumped the funding priority for school libraries from 2012 to 2014. This critical gaffe cost Washington school librarians two years of legislative support.

This simple anecdote illustrates the necessity of constant advocacy. When decision makers realize school library advocates are not going away, *regardless of whether or not these board members or legislators are strong library supporters*, they recognize the importance of working together to achieve what is best for students.

Authentic Advocates Arrive Unexpectedly

Nothing speaks more significantly toward support for libraries than the unsolicited and unexpected voice of members of the school community. Often such allies are not readily known to the school librarian. Most often these are the voices of students or parents, or sometimes fellow teachers.

What for some may appear even the slightest of gestures—such as finding the perfect book, Web site, or resource—may have a huge impact on an individual student or family and will result in a valuable advocate for the school library. Never underestimate who can become an advocate. Find ways to meet needs of constituents and share treasures with those who can ultimately influence the school library program.

The commitment to advocate for the school library from outside the ranks of school librarians themselves cannot be staged. These voices must ring true; thus, finding and developing these supporters is essential. They must have personal experience and a reason to become advocates, and school librarians are key to providing those experiences.

Advocates Are Collaborative Allies

It would be wonderful if every school library had parents, students, fellow teachers, and community members who stood up and spoke out on the value of the school library. In reality, most school librarians have only a few genuinely strong supporters they can call on to promote the library cause.

One of the most strategic acts a librarian can use to increase support is to work in collaboration with as many members of the school community as possible. For example, the school librarian who volunteers to assume responsibility (including designing assignments/lessons, grading, and recording) for the fifth-grade literacy standard or curriculum on nonfiction text features may develop a strong advocacy link with that teacher. The school librarian can then leverage this effort by sharing these assignments with parents and principals. School librarian Doug Achterman aptly states, "If you want to get to collaborate, you have to step into those leadership shoes first and establish yourself as a leader that somebody would want to collaborate with" (Achterman 2007). Once successful collaboration develops, it can be very beneficial to building library advocacy.

Advocacy Must Be Formally Recorded and Promoted

Look to those friends in the publishing business for great models on how many ways one message can be delivered. Walk through the Exhibit Hall at any library conference and observe the marketing strategies librarians could borrow to highlight the school library program. Publishers create posters, bookmarks, badges, magnets, and any number of paraphernalia using the cover illustration of a single book they are promoting. Why not use this same strategy to promote a unique event or evidence of marked academic improvement? Librarians can record data—for example, the skills and achievement gained during library curriculum lessons or research—and share results with principals, classroom teachers, and parents. The same results or data can be shared in multiple formats: library newsletters, grades for classroom teachers, or the library report to the principal.

Advocates Must Anticipate Change

Optimistic anticipation stands to showcase the school library. Whether it is the latest research in education or libraries, trends in curriculum and support services, educational technology, or change on a more global front, the school librarian who optimistically promotes inevitable change is seen as a cutting-edge change agent.

Technology changes daily; the library, as one of the technology hubs of the school, stands at the forefront of these changes. It is unrealistic for school librarians to assume responsibility for bringing the latest technology to all school library patrons. Instead, it is paramount to selectively anticipate and optimistically embrace and promote appropriate technology that the librarian can capably model. The focus should be on what improves student learning.

Advocacy Is about Access for All

One of the most important services a school library program provides is the *equitable access* of services, resources, technology, and other print material to the entire school community. This is core to the essence of a school library program, and school librarians often assume that this is naturally understood by members of the school community. But nothing should be assumed. When it comes to demonstrating the value of a school library program, the mantra of "equitable access" cannot be understated. It is imperative that the equitability of these services be constantly and publicly promoted in a way that helps decision makers understand the significance of the school library.

Advocates Bring Stories to Life

A newly retired librarian with tears in her eyes recently related this simple story on her last day at school: A young man she hardly recognized timidly approached her in the library and explained, "I'm [Ian], remember me? You were my librarian all through high school. I'm a senior at the U now. In college I've had to write so many research papers! If it hadn't been for some of the things you showed me about [how to find] research, I would've been lost. It's just. . . . I read about your retirement in the [news]paper this week and I just wanted to tell you that" (JoAnn Chinn, personal communication, 2009).

Anecdotes like these bring library stories to life and provide an enriched tapestry of detail to the dry list of data and facts used to support the value of the school librarian and the library. Such anecdotes when delivered by first-person storytellers pack a punch and create human connections. Whenever possible, particularly in formal advocacy presentations, use a personal story or anecdote to punctuate evidential data and bring humanity to activism. Collect such stories and keep them available.

A library is a fluid source of information, materials, and resources that remains viable only through the foresight and oversight of a professional librarian. New technologies can be managed, updated, shared, promoted, and connected to resources and learning needs with the insights of a professional librarian. Without a librarian, the library has no "voice." School librarians must be mindful of these facts as they work to develop a culture of advocacy.

Grassroots Advocacy

"Grassroots advocacy is a cornerstone of the democratic process" (Chrastka 2011). One never knows from where support and alliances may come. The highly publicized, high-profile Spokane Moms' story began simply when one mother walked down the hall of her child's school and saw the library dark, locked, and closed.

Grassroots advocacy ranges from simple acts to grand movements that often take on a life of their own. Grassroots advocacy does not necessarily culminate in something as tangible and far reaching as passage of legislation. Nor does it typically organize into a statewide or national movement. Grassroots advocacy can simply provide alliance, support, and an external voice promoting the value of school libraries.

Grassroots advocacy should never be underestimated. At the heart of any such activism is the fact that to viewers and bystanders these advocates are seen as unbiased and reliable spokespersons. Grassroots advocates are seen as caring, selfless individuals, committed to a higher service, and, by that very fact, they showcase the importance of their cause—in this case, the school library. They speak from personal experience, self-driven motivation, and sincere belief in the cause for which they speak.

Authentic grassroots efforts evolve organically from a perfect storm of need, passion, and commitment. When a school community is fortunate enough to have such a movement, the school library community must embrace and serve these efforts tirelessly. It may be necessary to provide everything from croissants to data for grassroots activists involved in promoting the school library program.

Developing an Advocacy Plan

Adding a small act of advocacy to everyday library activities can bring results and helps build toward a more extended, in-depth plan over time. In fact, the impact of simple acts of advocacy may be surprising enough that it will seem natural to establish a deeper level of ongoing advocacy. Any of the following will highlight events of learning already happening in the school library and serve as simply ways to share various library events, initiatives, and learning connections. Nearly all of these acts of advocacy can be conducted electronically or virtually as well as in print. As always, use of a positive tone within any presentation promotes the universal library's credo of "Welcome All."

Important note: For each of the following examples, it is imperative that the event, activity, promotional idea, educational opportunity, or academic skill be presented as part of the school library program taught by a highly qualified, certificated school librarian.

Parent–Teacher Connection

The strongest ally the librarian has is that of the parent advocate. Connecting to parents and families is critical, and parents can be a school's greatest advocates. One important form of communication to consider is the PTA newsletter. Commit to a brief, one-paragraph, "What's New in the Library" column in the family, school, or community newsletter. Include any of the following unique to the individual school or library:

- Literacy and reading motivation ideas for parents
- Creative learning activities happening in the library
- Helpful parenting ideas (Internet safety, legal downloading, Internet search strategies)
- Suggested family read-alouds
- Library curriculum of 21st-century skills
- Suggested birthday or holiday literature purchases
- Announcements/requests for volunteers
- Help parents talk to children about appropriate selections (For additional ideas on appropriate selection, see H. Adams, "Reaching Out to Parents.")

Monthly Administrative Reports

A monthly administrative report is vital to the future of the school library program. *Impact on student learning* must be the first priority and primary focus. Send copies to principals, the library administrator, and the district curriculum director. Include:

- Data, data, data:
  - Impact studies (Kachel 2011)
  - Standardized test components taught in the library

  - ◦ Grades/lesson results taught in the library
  - ◦ Number of books checked out (include research on importance of "choice")
  - ◦ Number of books/material added to collection
  - ◦ Number of classes visiting the library
- Library curriculum impact on high-stakes standardized test scores
- Library curriculum of 21st-century skills
- Collaboration with classroom teachers
- Content-area skills taught
- Unique units of study
- Lesson plans/curriculum aligned with content area standards
- Lesson plans/curriculum aligned with school/district curriculum
- Reading and literacy activities in place
- Events held in the library
- Results of how budgets have positively affected resources
- Lists of online resources
- "Famous" visitors (see "Guest Speakers")

Administrators have a human side. Along with student data, consider also including quotes or anecdotes from library students, parents, or fellow teachers. Never underestimate the power of "story." Use exit slips and collected reflections from students about what or how they learned during their work in the library.

Always end the principal's report or newsletter on a positive note. Be sure the *majority* of these reports contain no requests or issues of complaint; as a result, administrators will begin to welcome your communiqué. Further, this proactive advocacy may ensure an ally when tough decisions threaten the library program. (For a sample principal's report, see Kaaland and Nickerson, "Notes from the Bullet Train.")

Library Newsletter—or e-Newsletter

Those who enjoy writing may wish to commit to a regularly published library newsletter or e-newsletter. Pull any of the ideas listed in this chapter for the library newsletter. It's best to commit to quarterly at first and use electronic versions whenever possible. Include interesting anecdotes—large and small—and stories of events and happenings in the library.

Guest Speakers

In the commitment to ensuring that the school library is the hub of the school, guest speakers in the library can highlight that fact simply by their presence. As always, consider guests who may also affect student achievement and leverage results. Consider other guest speakers with a dual intent of highlighting the library program. These may include:

- Author or illustrator visits
- School superintendent or school board member
- Local famous community members or business persons

- Local legislators (Hint: They are particularly receptive when running for office or when photo ops are offered.)

Publishing Students' Work

What parents or guardians do not love to see their children's name in print? Multiple resources, both online and print, can offer opportunities for children to compete or submit their original works for publication. Whether the librarian teaches the skills involved in these publications or simply conducts a "Call for Submissions," sending student work in for publication encourages students to think of themselves as authors and sends a powerful literary message to the school community at large.

Want quicker results? Consider self-publishing student illustrations and writing. Whether the theme is library curriculum, literary clubs, or promotional programs, librarians should highlight their program when student work is reproduced and published, emphasizing the information and literacy learning. Examples may include:

- Kindergartners creating recipes for class cookbooks
- Alphabet books created on any particular topic studied
- Collaborative research projects
- All-school poetry, essay, or art contest where everyone's a winner

Student Galleries

Student work on display, both written and illustrated, provides wonderful exposure for the school library. Volunteer to display student work at key locations:

- School board meeting room
- Central administration building
- Local public office buildings
- Voting/election locations (have students write about current issues and post at election polls)

Critical to these exhibits is a high-profile library and librarian.

Student Products and Productions

Student assignments conducted in collaboration with classroom teachers or solely in the library may provide greater visibility for the importance of the school library program *when librarians share these works.* Displaying student work in the library is important; however, only those who enter the library will see this work. Consider sharing student work on a greater scale outside the walls of the library. Post on the school Web site; better still, ask to submit to district-wide student work exhibit.

Library-Centered All-School or Community Events

Activities—grand or small—that librarians regularly perform need to be shared, highlighting the school library program. Joyce Valenza regularly shares unique ideas for grand promotion of library events on her Web site and *School Library Journal*'s Web site (Neverendingsearch), such as her recent "Read It First," Valenza's schoolwide promotion for reading books before they become movies, which includes a fun "Read It First" pledge and sign-up for new movies-from-books.

Even a typical librarian activity such as weeding books can serve to highlight the library and involve the greater school community, such as L. J. Martin's Ugly Book Cover contest that brought students and teachers alike into the library to judge books for weeding (Martin 2011).

Building an Extended Advocacy Plan

After implementing small-scale acts of advocacy, individuals realize how well these actions produced results and had an impact on support. As a result, it seems more probable to practice advocacy on a greater scale and at a deeper level. With pressing concerns over budget shortfalls and staffing issues that threaten resources for school libraries, the district library leaders must initiate a district-wide comprehensive advocacy plan. For a district-wide plan to be truly successful, the majority of the district's librarians must not just contribute and be involved, they must also embrace a culture of advocacy in their daily work. (See chapter 3 by Ann Martin.)

The purpose of a district-wide plan is to inform the greater school community of the value of supporting and maintaining a strong school library program. The ultimate goal then is to first reeducate all stakeholders, informing them of the characteristics of a strong, 21st-century library program, and then establish a commitment to maintaining it. In developing such a plan, this goal must become the foundation.

As with all such promotional work, although it begins and ends with the hard work of librarians, greater success is attained when members of the school community at large become involved: parents, students, fellow teachers, and particularly administrators. At the onset, it is imperative that the district-wide advocacy plan include outside spokespersons, so it is important to gather contact information of school community members willing to be involved. In this way, whenever possible, these advocates (outside the immediate circle of librarians) can become the public *voice* and *face* for school library advocacy.

A district-wide advocacy plan begins with librarians composing a broad mission or vision statement that succinctly describes the library program and its unique qualities. As librarians begin to reach out to community members for enlisting greater support, this vision or mission statement flags all correspondence, represents a unified voice, and delivers a message of unification for the library program district-wide. As always, at the heart of this vision must be how the school library affects student achievement.

Once a vision/mission statement has been composed, four actions follow somewhat simultaneously: (1) Determine school librarian involvement, district-wide; (2) Determine key program content information to disseminate; (3) Establish an information dissemination plan (to whom and where); and (4) Create an advocacy timeline or calendar of planned events (one to five years) for continuously and strategically disseminating information regarding the school library program.

Determine and Communicate School Library Involvement

In smaller districts with one or fewer librarians, it is impossible to serve on all district committees. Strategically then, these librarians must carefully select committee work with the greatest impact by major decision-makers. For example, it would behoove the librarian to join the curriculum selection committee with a curriculum director under whose purview major curriculum decisions are made.

Larger districts provide greater flexibility and opportunities to affect district-wide decisions by dispersing committee work among the district's librarians. There should be frank conversations that result in matching individual librarian expertise and dispositions to provide input for select committees and with district administrators who will most likely influence school library programs. Strategically, consider the following: schools whose principals are most influential and committees whose work is disseminated to the broadest audience range.

Ensure librarian representation for the following district initiatives, typically, committee membership:

- Selecting a new superintendent
- Selecting new content area curriculum
- Promoting individual school board candidates
- Negotiating contracts
- Selecting technology
- Making union decisions (serve on the executive boards)

Consider: *How can the library program expand influence district-wide?*

Identify School Library Program Content

Determine key content addressed through library instruction and communicate such information with decision makers, such as the school library and librarian role in

- Collaboration and work with content area standards-based instruction and evidence-based practices
- Literacy and reading advocacy programs
- Technology
- Information literacy
- Information management
- Research skills and inquiry
- Job-readiness skills
- Author visits, special library programs
- Special-needs student needs (English-language learning, special education, gifted)
- Cyber-curriculum (cyber-bullying, identify safekeeping, cyber predators)
- Grants, awards, promotional bids

Consider: *What might key decision-makers not know about the library program? What misconceptions or stereotypes need to be overcome?*

Orchestrate Information Dissemination

What institutional or organizational bodies need information on the impact of school libraries and why? Recognizing the needs of the recipient audience is central to establishing a district-wide plan. Advocates must ask themselves: *What is it this individual or organization needs that the school library can uniquely provide?* Responses that are both formal and informal should address this question. These may include:

A. Formal Presentations:
- School board
- Administrators' meeting
- Community clubs and organizations
- District-wide PTA

B. Virtual Presence:
- Design, update, and promote library Web presence
- Promote new software or educational technology tools
- 24/7 connectivity
- Databases
- Cyber-curriculum
- Connecting to the world at large

Consider: *How many ways and with the use of what tools can information on the positive academic impact of school libraries be disseminated?*

Create an Advocacy Timeline/Calendar

When to make large-scale presentations on the school library is nearly as important as what information is disseminated. School districts have benchmarks for decision making, particularly budgetary decisions. Creating a matrix recording key decision-makers, what they need to know about the school library to make informed decisions, and in what formats that information will be presented or disseminated will likely determine key timeline events.

Consider: *When is the best time to disseminate information on the impact of school libraries to make the biggest impression?*

Jamie Daniel's Story

Jamie was just 21 when, after completing her undergraduate and master's degrees and all but the final class for her state school library certification, she was hired for her first school library position. Inspired at an early age by her high school librarian, Sarah Applegate, Jamie was driven and she had a vision for her school library program. Having grown up in the digital world, she taught her peers to access sites, skills, and other technologies that were new to seasoned educators. Within short order, Jamie became actively involved in the state library organization. Within months of beginning her first job, the Washington Library Media Association (WLMA) president asked her to combine these technology skills and her school library knowledge to testify before the state legislature regarding educational technology legislation. Standing confidently before a crowded room of legislators, Jamie demonstrated technologies that had senators and representatives poised on the edge of their seats. At the end of her testimony, questioning from legislators lasted another 45 minutes as Jamie confidently taught legislators new technologies. Jamie's testimonial profoundly affected legislation, and she was able to frame her presentation within the context of the school library program. Jamie's story serves as a model for powerful school library advocacy.

Profundity, One Final Word

In order to make a lasting impact on decision makers, a district-wide advocacy plan must include profound, perhaps even mind-altering, new knowledge about the world inside today's school library program. Presenting a list—whether of actions, activities, curriculum, or teaching—regardless of how impressive or detailed, is not enough to ensure that decision makers will be moved enough to commit to sustained support of school libraries. Decision makers need to be wowed. It can happen incrementally or as a lightning strike, but it must be profound. When decision makers move forward in their chairs and lean in to hear the story, profundity happens.

The impact of a district-wide advocacy plan is unique to the district it serves, but through such efforts positive results will occur and serendipitously strengthen a district's library program. It brings the district librarians together for a common cause. Working together to develop a plan opens conversations and increases colleague communication concerning what transpires in every library. Furthermore, proper advocacy prior to disasters saves programs. Most importantly, these combined efforts result in safeguarding strong library programs for students. (For more details on establishing and implementing a district-wide school library plan, see chapter 3.)

> ### Additional Advocacy Tools
>
> These additional resources are available in the appendix:
>
> "Use This Page: Advocacy 101." *School Library Monthly* (February 2012): 2. See page 107.
>
> "Use This Page: Advocacy Planning: Vision, Voice, Visibility, and Vigilance." *School Library Monthly* (January 2012): 2. See page 108.
>
> "Use This Page: Library Advocacy through Teaching and Learning." *School Library Monthly* (January 2010): 2. See page 109.
>
> "Use This Page: Data-Driven Program Development: A Quick Guide." *School Library Monthly* (November 2011): 2. See page 106.

In Summary

Whether the level of readiness is to embrace advocacy on a full scale or simply dip one's toe in the water, the library program and all its patrons will benefit from acts of advocacy. Most important is sharing the impact of the library on student learning and the successes and achievements with the school community at large. Whether large-scale or incremental small acts, it is the way in which librarians approach, frame, and share what they do every day that makes the advocacy difference.

References

Achterman, Doug. "The Sower." *School Library Journal* 53, no. 10 (2007): 50.

Adams, H. "Reaching Out to Parents." *School Library Monthly* 27, no. 8 (May/June 2011): 48.

American Association of School Librarians. *AASL Advocacy Toolkit*. 2011. http://www.ala.org/ala/mgrps/divs/aasl/aaslissues/toolkits/aasladvocacy.cfm (accessed January 7, 2012).

Chrastka, John. "Grassroots Advocacy Training Session to Cover Federal Issues, How to Effectively Reach Congress." 2011. http://americanlibrariesmagazine.org/ala-members-blog/grassroots-advocacy-training-session-cover-federal-issues-how-effectively-reach-con (accessed November 11, 2011).

Harada, Violet H., and Joan M. Yoshina. *Assessing for Learning: Librarians and Teachers as Partners*, 2nd ed. Santa Barbara, Calif.: Libraries Unlimited, 2010.

Kaaland, C., and D. Nickerson. "Notes from the Bullet Train: Communication as a Key to Administrative Support." *School Library Monthly* 26, no. 8 (April 2010): 45.

Kachel, Debra E. "School Library Research Summarized: A Graduate Class Project." Mansfield University, 2011. http://libweb.mansfield.edu/upload/kachel/ImpactStudy.pdf (accessed September 30, 2011).

Kerr, E. "Engaging the Decision-Makers and the Influencers." *Teacher Librarian* 38, no. 3 (February 2011): 69.

Martin, L. J. "Needing a Weeding: How Judging a Book by Its Cover Can Help." *Library Media Connection* 30, no. 2 (October 2011): 18.

School Libraries Work! Research Foundation Paper. Scholastic, 2008. http://listbuilder.scholastic.com/content/stores/LibraryStore/pages/images/SLW3.pdf (accessed November 13, 2011).

TRAILS (Tool for Real-time Assessment of Information Literacy Skills). Kent State University. 2012. http://www.trails-9.org/ (accessed January 3, 2012).

"Use This Page: Advocacy 101." *School Library Monthly* 28, no. 5 (February 2012): 2.

"Use This Page: Advocacy Planning: Vision, Voice, Visibility, and Vigilance." *School Library Monthly* 28, no. 4 (January 2012): 2.

"Use This Page: Assessment Tool: Levels of Communication, Cooperation, and Collaboration with Teachers." *School Library Media Activities Monthly* 23, no. 2 (October 2006): 2.

"Use This Page: Data-Driven Program Development: A Quick Guide." *School Library Monthly* 28, no. 2 (November 2011): 2.

"Use This Page: Library Advocacy through Teaching and Learning." *School Library Monthly* 27, no. 4 (January 2010): 2.

"Use This Page: Taking Action: Saving School Libraries." *School Library Monthly* 27, no. 5 (February 2011): 2.

Additional Resources:

Abrams, Stephen. "School Library Advocacy." *Stephen's Lighthouse*. http://stephenslighthouse.com/2011/05/09/school-library-advocacy/ (accessed December 29, 2011).

Alire, C. "Front-Line Advocacy." *American Libraries* 41, no. 3 (2010): 6.

Allen, Dixie. "We Are Not Alone." *School Library Monthly* 27, no. 1 (2010): 48–49.

Anderson, M. "Advocacy in Action: When Company Comes." *Internet@Schools* 13, no. 1 (2006): 32–34.

Berry, J. "Students Sound Off about Their Schools." *Library Journal* 124, no. 18 (1999): 46.

Beyers, Catherine. "Lean on One Another." *School Library Media Activities Monthly* 22, no. 7 (2006): 47–48.

Campbell, Pam. "Why Would Anyone Want to Follow the Leader?" *School Library Media Activities Monthly* 25, no. 8 (2009): 52–54.

Dougherty, R. "Library Advocacy: One Message, One Voice." *American Libraries* 42, no. 5 (2011): 46–50.

Everhart, Nancy. "Leadership: School Library Media Specialists as Effective School Leaders." *Knowledge Quest* 35, no. 4 (2007): 55–57.

Fields, K. "Advancing Advocacy." *American Libraries* 38, no. 10 (2007): 8.

Foote, C. "Everyday Advocacy." *School Library Journal* 56, no. 8 (2010): 28.

Gay, Patrick D. "Grass Roots Advocacy." *School Library Monthly* 28, no. 5 (February 2009): 30–32.

Hand, D. "What Can Teacher-Librarians Do to Promote Their Work and the School Library Media Program? Keep Everyone in the Loop: Constant Advocacy." *Teacher Librarian* 36, no. 2 (2008): 26–27.

Harvey II, Carl. "Being Tactical with Advocacy." *Teacher Librarian* 37, no. 4 (2010): 89–90.

Hawkins, A. "Teaching Advocacy and Making Change." *Leadership for Student Activities* 36, no. 7 (2008): 12–15.

Johns, Sara Kelly. "School Librarians Taking the Leadership Challenge." *School Library Monthly* 27, no. 4 (2011): 37–39.

Kaaland, Christie. "A Campaign of Gratitude." *School Library Media Activities Monthly* 25, no. 9 (2009): 52–53.

Kaaland, Christie. "Creating a District-Wide Advocacy Plan, Part 1." *School Library Monthly* 28, no. 4 (December 2011): 29–31.

Kaaland, Christie. "Creating a District-Wide Advocacy Plan, Part 2." *School Library Monthly* 28, no. 4 (January 2012): 29–31.

Kaaland, Christie. "Proactive Advocacy: 'Emergency Preparedness' for the School Library. *School Library Monthly* 27, no. 4 (2011): 49–51.

Kaaland, Christie. "Recruitment to the Profession: A Form of Advocacy." *School Library Monthly* 26, no. 10 (2010): 44–46.

Kaaland, Christie. "Saving Your School Library." *School Library Monthly* 26, no. 5 (January 2010): 7–9.

Kramer, P. "Evidence + Assessment = Advocacy." *Teacher Librarian* 37, no. 3 (2010): 27–30.

Lance, K. C. "What Research Tells Us about the Importance of School Libraries." *Teacher Librarian* 30, no. 1 (2002): 76.

Lehman, K. "Promoting Library Advocacy and Information Literacy from an 'Invisible Library.'" *Teacher Librarian* 29, no. 4 (2002): 27–30.

Levitov, Deborah. "Advocacy Links . . . Tools to Use." *School Library Media Activities Monthly* 25, no. 7 (2009): 4.

Levitov, Deborah. "How to Manage Information Overload." *School Library Media Activities Monthly* 24, no. 7 (2008): 4.

Levitov, Deborah. "One Library Media Specialist's Journey to Understanding Advocacy: A Tale of Transformation." *Knowledge Quest* 36, no. 1 (2007): 28–31.

Levitov, Deborah. "Make It Meaningful." *School Library Media Activities Monthly* 28, no. 5 (February 2012): 4.

Levitov, Deborah. *Perspectives of School Administrators Related to School Library Media Programs after Participating in an Online Course, "School Library Advocacy for Administrators."* PhD diss., University of Missouri, Columbia, 2009.

Levitov, Deborah. "The Many Roads to Advocacy." *School Library Media Activities Monthly* 24, no. 6 (2008): 4.

Levitov, Deborah. "The School Librarian as an Advocacy Leader." In *Many Faces of Advocacy*. Edited by Sharon Coatney. Santa Barbara, Calif.: Libraries Unlimited, 2010.

Levitov, Deborah D. "Tools for Survival." *School Library Monthly* 28, no. 4 (January 2012): 4.

Loertscher, David. "Advocacy through Statistics, Research, and Major Reports." *Teacher Librarian* 36, no. 2 (2008): 46.

Loertscher, David, and Elizabeth Marcoux. "On Learning from the Best, Becoming the Best, and Being the Best." *Teacher Librarian* 38, no. 4 (2011): 6–7, 75.

Logan, Debra Kay. "Being Heard . . . Advocacy + Evidence + Students = IMPACT!" *School Library Media Activities Monthly* 23, no. 1 (2006): 46–48.

Marcoux, Elizabeth. "Advocacy and the Teacher-Librarian." *Teacher Librarian* 36, no. 2 (2008): 6–7, 84.

Martin, Ann M. "Data Driven Leadership." *School Library Monthly* 28, no. 2 (November 2011): 31–33.

Martin, Ann M. *Seven Steps to an Award-Winning School Library Program*. 2nd ed. Santa Barbara, Calif.: Libraries Unlimited, 2012.

McGhee, Marla. "Having a School Library Work Plan." *School Library Monthly* 28, no. 6 (March 2012): 32–34.

Michie, J. S., and B. W. Chaney. *Improving Literacy through School Libraries Evaluation*. Washington, D.C.: U.S. Government Printing Office, 2005.

Price, B. "Budgets and School Libraries: Rethinking Priorities." *Teacher Librarian* 30, no. 5 (2003): 63.

Ray, Mark. "Big Picture Advocacy: Making Fifteen Minutes Count." *School Library Monthly* 28, no. 6 (March 2012): 29–31.

Read Burkman, Amy. "A Practical Approach to Marketing the School Library Program." *Library Media Connection* 23, no. 3 (2004): 42–43.

Roscello, Frances. "Standards Implementation: A Planned Advocacy Campaign." *School Libraries in Canada* 23, no. 1 (2003): 9–13.

Schulz, C. "Developing an Advocacy Plan for the School Library Media Center." *Book Report* 18, no. 3 (1999): 19–22.

Shantz, D. "Program Advocacy: What Is the Purpose of Program Advocacy? Why Should Teacher-Librarians Be Involved with Program Advocacy?" *Emergency Librarian* 21, no. 3 (1994): 22–25.

Solomon, C. "School Librarian's Role Shifting from Storyteller to Data Expert; Emphasis on Managing Information Resources of Digital Age." *Seattle Times* (February 26, 2004): B2.

Streatfield, D., and S. Markless. "Impact Evaluation, Advocacy and Ethical Research: Some Issues for National Strategy Development?" *Library Review* 60, no. 4 (2011).

Stripling, Barbara. "The Dance of Leadership and Advocacy." *Knowledge Quest* 36, no. 1 (2007): 54–55.

Tarulli, L. "Taking the Leadership Initiative: How You Can Fight the Budget Cut Battle." *School Libraries in Canada* 24, no. 3 (2004): 39.

Tilley, Carol. "The True Value of the Work We Do." *School Library Monthly* 27, no. 8 (2011): 45–47.

Todardo, J., and P. Wong. "Advocacy at the Front Lines." *American Libraries* 41, no. 1 (2010): 80.

Underwood, Linda. *A Case Study of Four School Library Media Specialists' Leadership in Louisiana*. West Virginia University, 2003.

Young, Terrence E., Jr. "Marketing Your School Library Media Center: What We Can Learn from National Bookstores." *Library Media Connection* 28, no. 6 (2010): 18–20.

Zmuda, Allison. "Six Steps to Saving Your School Library Program." *School Library Media Activities Monthly* 27, no. 5 (February 2010): 45–48.

Zmuda, Allison. "Where Does Your Authority Come From? Empowering the Library Media Specialist as a True Partner in Student Achievement." *School Library Media Activities Monthly* 23, no. 1 (September 2006): 19–22.

5

School Library Legislative Advocacy Defined

Christie Kaaland and Debra E. Kachel

Frankly, trying to educate elected officials without asking for something specific is like trying to educate a middle-schooler without telling them it will be on the test. It goes in one ear and out the other.

—Stephanie Vance, June 2010

School library advocacy has been defined as "an on-going process of building partnerships so that others will act for and with you, turning passive support into educated action in support of the school library program. It begins with a vision and a plan for the school library program that is then matched to the agenda and priorities of the stakeholders" (American Association of School Librarians). From this broad definition, we can propose that school library *legislative* advocacy begins with the development of a relationship between school library advocates—librarians and beyond—and legislative decision makers.

Key to this relationship building is education—in terms of educating legislators about what it means to provide equitable school library programs that include instruction for students, as well as educating oneself with regard to what is important to legislators. This implies clear and consistent communication, research, and a rapport in which the librarian is the expert, viewed as a trusted, authoritative, and credible source of information representing a group of the legislator's constituency who value and believe the same thing. Legislators are most concerned with representing the views of their constituents—constituents who will vote for them—and they need to know how many people support a specific issue. Therefore, *effective* legislative advocacy must be organized and widespread—selling the library position to others and delivering numbers of constituents to the legislator. Simply stating why school library programs are needed will not move legislators into action until they are shown large-scale constituent support.

Why Is Legislative Advocacy Needed? Why Now?

There has never been a better time *or a more critical time* than the present for advocates to work with legislative decision makers to promote legislation that supports a strong school library program. Throughout the nation, in each state and in each school district, decision makers are struggling with what to cut as they try to reduce debt and improve financial stability. School library programs, where not mandated by contract or law, are at the top of the cut list because they are expensive and not required, and cuts may affect the least number of staff, if staff must be furloughed.

Without regulations and mandates, school library programs range from totally nonexistent to programs that are fully staffed with a standards-based, instructional curriculum; accessible facilities with an abundance of print and digital resources; and up-to-date computers with access to other technologies. The decision to fund school libraries can even vary within a school district, as many districts have adopted site-based management as an acceptable business model. Only through legislative and policy-making efforts at the state or federal level will some level of equity of library service be achieved for all students across the state or nation.

Yet more is expected of today's student-learners. Employers across the nation are urging schools to better prepare students with 21st-century skills so companies can be globally competitive and productive. In 2009, a study of businesses whose organizations had at least 25 percent new employees who had two or more years of college found that employers sought the following skills in new workers:

- The ability to communicate effectively, orally and in writing (89%)
- Critical thinking and analytical reasoning skills (81%)
- The ability to analyze and solve complex problems (75%)
- Teamwork skills and the ability to collaborate with others in diverse group settings (71%)
- The ability to innovate and be creative (70%)
- The ability to locate, organize, and evaluate information from multiple sources (68%) (Hart Research Associates 2010, 2)

Quality school library programs with full-time, certified librarians teach these 21st-century skills. In over 22 states, school library impact studies have correlated higher standardized reading test scores with quality school library programs (Kachel 2011). In fact, quality school library programs may play an even greater role in providing academic support to those students who come from economically disadvantaged backgrounds. Despite abundant research, reductions and eliminations of school librarians and library programs are resulting in huge inequities in learning opportunities for students, creating an access gap between schools in wealthier communities and those with high levels of poverty. A recent study found that by examining correlations between school library characteristics and student poverty, there were "consistent and statistically significant differences between libraries housed in schools with low and high concentrations of students living in poverty." In other words, students who need school library services the most have the least—in staff, resources, and library access (Pribesh, Gavigan, and Dickinson 2011, 43–60).

Politics in Schools: What Is Acceptable?

Most state school library organizations have an advocacy or legislative committee usually made up of only a handful of librarians. However, the work needed to influence legislation is monumental. Rallying librarians across the state to become activists is imperative to successful legislative results. Most state school library organizations already have resources prepared and LISTSERVs in place that can be used to quickly reach a large number of people. Strong, committed individuals are needed to lead the charge.

Although state organizations may provide access to organizational LISTSERVs, advocacy committee members should create advocacy lists of school library advocates who will contact their legislators when action is posted. These contacts should include more than just librarians: parents, business leaders, and other library-friendly activists. Whenever possible, personal or nonschool e-mail should be used to contact advocates on library legislative issues. Often, school districts disapprove of using district e-mail services funded through taxpayer dollars to "lobby" a political agenda, even though it might be in the best interest of all students and schools. The district may even have a written policy pertaining to this as part of their Internet Use Policy. However, check with a school official, as some e-mails may be allowable, such as encouraging teachers and staff to contact their legislators about passing a bill that has increased funding for schools. Another option is to send an initial e-mail to staff members requesting that they respond with a personal e-mail address so that future e-mails related to school library advocacy will go to their personal accounts. Follow district Internet use policies in posting advocacy-related information on the library Web site. It is always best to ask first!

The same applies to letter writing. Use plain stationary, not the letterhead of the school unless thanking a legislator for visiting the school. Writing letters, especially those sent to a legislator's local district office, is still an appropriate thing to do. Mail sent to the U.S. Congress and now many state capitals is screened via x-ray machines, so letters often take longer to reach legislators. For tips on proper letter format and letter-writing etiquette, check the Internet (Robert Longley's "Letters to Congress" *About.com Guide*, http://usgovinfo.about.com/od/uscongress/a/letterscongress.htm).

What Librarians Need to Know about Legislators and the Legislative Process

School librarians need to first learn who their state and federal legislators are and conduct basic research to learn about each person individually (see figure 5.1). School librarians may actually have two sets of state legislators—legislators who represent where the librarian lives and legislators who represent the area in which the librarian's school is located. Understand that legislators want to hear from their constituents, so librarians need to be careful to use the school address in correspondence directed to the school's legislators and use their home address when contacting legislators who represent their home area. However, it's great to be able to contact several legislators with your message: one as resident and voter, the other as the librarian in the district a legislator represents. Librarians should clearly identify themselves when using a school or work address by stating in the message, "I am the school librarian at XYZ school" so that the legislator has a point of reference.

The American Library Association (ALA) maintains a site called the Legislative Action Center (http://capwiz.com/ala/home/) where librarians can find federal and state legislators' names and links to their Web sites, as well as the latest library legislative

Legislator Research for Successful Advocacy

Previous profession/education background

Hometown

Family/personal information (i.e, hobbies, where their children attend school)

Committee work

Seniority or ranking among peer legislators

Topics of supported and passed legislation

Bills introduced

Votes on legislation

For state legislators, the school districts they represent

When their term ends (reelection?)

Fig. 5.1. Learning about legislators.

issues. This site also provides preformatted e-mail messages where one can simply add contact information and hit "submit." However, know that legislators today are flooded with preformatted e-mails, so this is primarily used to show numbers of constituents interested in an issue. For greater impact, a personal e-mail or letter, phone call, or visit makes a much stronger impression. In addition, library advocates can create their own message and ask others on e-mail distribution lists to copy the text and forward the message from their e-mail. This works especially well when asking teachers to send e-mails on behalf of a library issue. If the librarian creates the text, it is more likely to be e-mailed.

The biggest faux pas people make is e-mailing or writing the wrong legislator—either contacting a state legislator about a piece of federal legislation or vice versa. An instant loss of credibility! Obviously, when asking for support on federal legislation, focus on U.S. congressmen and congresswomen. Current federal issues related to school libraries include the reauthorization of the Elementary and Secondary Education Act (ESEA) and the Strengthening Kids' Interest in Learning and Libraries Act (SKILLs). Librarians can keep current on federal legislation by going to the blog called "District Dispatch" maintained by the ALA Washington office. Select "School Libraries" for the type of library (http://www.districtdispatch.org/?cat=11).

Most legislators' Web sites provide everything on the topics covered in the balance of this chapter. As the librarian completes this research, she or he may find topics of mutual concern or other personal connections. These are important to reference in correspondence or when meeting legislators face to face.

What Is the Message or "The Ask"?

Usually federal legislative advocacy is directed by a library organization or a regional team of librarians and other advocates such as the ALA or the American Association of School Librarians (AASL). These national organizations employ lobbyists who have expertise in what legislation to target and what additional legislation is needed. ALA/AASL's Washington office (http://www.ala.org/ala/aboutala/offices/wo/index.cfm) is operated by lobbyists who advise at the federal level. This Legislative Action Center provides information about ALA and AASL's recent legislative actions.

Sample Legislative Platforms of State School Library Associations

Florida http://www.floridamedia.org/resource/resmgr/advoc_legislative/2011_fame_platform.pdf

Wisconsin http://www.wla.lib.wi.us/legis/priorities.htm

South Carolina http://www.statelibrary.sc.gov/View-document/232-South-Carolina-Libraries
-Legislative-Agenda-2007 (shows a combined approach-all types of libraries)

Fig. 5.2.   State legislative platforms.

At the state level, whether through connections with the school library organiza-tion or through an ad hoc group of dedicated librarians, activists can begin their own grassroots advocacy campaign. In either case, a collaborative approach is best to show strength in numbers and to plan the strategies for "The Ask."

It is critical that the advocacy group have an "Ask" or a request for the legislator to act on in behalf of school libraries. It is ineffective to visit legislators to simply inform them about library programs unless it is to invite them to a school visit. A more effec-tive advocacy campaign involves determining specifically what to ask the legislator. That being said, it is completely appropriate to visit a legislator to explain an issue or problem and ask the legislator for advice on strategies for resolving the problem. It is not a prerequisite to be an expert in government or a lobbyist to participate in legisla-tive advocacy. Most legislators love to give advice or help resolve constituents' issues when possible. Stephanie Vance, known as the "Advocacy Guru," works frequently with ALA issues and has useful books and free podcasts to help the advocacy leader-ship team (see Additional Resources).

In establishing "The Ask," consider both long-range and short-term objectives, un-derstanding they may be different. Although advocates might want a mandate that every school will employ a certified/licensed, full-time school librarian, that is not likely to happen quickly. Therefore, it is a long-range goal. However, advocates should consider what might be achievable in the short term that moves toward the ultimate long-range goal. For example, if a school code bill is being revised or amended, it may be a good time to try to add language about school libraries even if the language is not a mandate or does not involves funding. This is neither a requirement nor a funding issue. Fiscally neutral requests are generally easier, and are a good way to begin.

Some state school library organizations have well-developed legislative platforms, and some of them employ a part-time lobbyist to assist them (see figure 5.2). However, the legislative agenda does not need to be formal or lengthy. In fact, common sense dictates starting small to achieve small successes and build support among the librari-ans and library advocates the group represents.

Determining Which Legislators to Approach

Once "The Ask" is determined, if the advocacy effort is grassroots and does not have the advice or expertise of a lobbyist, the team should research potential legislators who are members of the Education Committees in both the House and Senate. Keep in mind that the controlling party at the time probably has a greater ability to pass or amend legislation than the minority party. Try to find a legislator with ties to libraries or who has passed library legislation in the past. Another option is to contact the state teachers' union for advice. All this becomes part of the research and preparation phase. Having a team to divide up this work load is most effective.

The most difficult thing to do is to find an individual legislator who is willing to commit to school libraries as one of their key areas of interest. Before legislation can happen, one individual legislator must step up to sponsor legislation. Two approaches may prove successful. The first is to call on known advocates. Historically, school librarians' greatest advocate at the national level has been Rhode Island senator Jack Reed. Senator Reed has been a strong library advocate for much of his career. Try to find who the most consistent library supporter is in your own state legislature. The second approach is to find candidates who are likely to sponsor legislation based on their personal interests, voting record, committee work, and personal interests.

Crafting the Message to Appeal to Politicians: The Language of Political Activism

It is easily recognized during the campaign season that politicians carefully select key phrases and terms that strike at the heart of voters. Similarly, after initially researching a particular legislator's area of interest, activists need to craft a message in ways that appeal to or catch the legislator's interest.

Three components to consider when addressing the language used for advocating political support are

- Advocates must learn a few key legislative terms, including but not limited to those that strategically spark legislators' interest (see figure 5.3).
- Advocates must appeal to the legislative interests of the politician they are courting (see figure 5.3). In this case, key language addresses specific legislative terms that may be unfamiliar or beyond typical school library language.
- Advocates should attend to educating legislators on the language of 21st-century school libraries.

It cannot be assumed that legislators will understand school library lingo (e.g., information literacy, inquiry, collection development, AASL, online catalogs, databases, media, collaboration).

Language of Legislation

Knowing the best tactics for influencing legislators requires a bit of homework. Legislators and legislative aides will recognize activists who have done their homework when advocates use key terms in their communication with legislators (see figure 5.3).

Visiting Legislators to Make "The Ask"

Preparing Handouts

Most legislators will not know about the voluminous body of statewide research studies that shows how robust school library programs with certified staffing correlates with improved student learning. Unfortunately, the school library field has been

LANGUAGE IS KEY

Advocates must consider language, focus, and priorities when enlisting legislators for library support. The following suggestions may help advocates gain a greater success in leveraging support based on the legislators' personal interests and political profiles. Following are several key political "buzz words," agendas and political interests. Adapt the suggested response to spark legislative language appropriate to individual needs of the legislator.

BACK TO BASICS:
Research indicates that students, particularly struggling readers, are more likely to show improved reading scores if provided with a variety of high interest reading material appealing to his or her unique reading preferences (Krashen 2004).

State-specific studies by Keith Curry Lance can also provide research of interest to a legislator's specific constituencies (Scholastic, 2008).

ENVIRONMENTALISM:
Libraries are the ultimate "recycling centers," checking out books, magazines, and other sources of information to multiple readers, saves natural resources and teaching kids to use digital resources and tools.

One single popular title for which the library distributes ten copies each, read by thirty readers can save paper equal to 100,000 pages of print. Multiply this by one library's collection and savings mount to over $100,000 in printed material; multiplied by the number of school district libraries and savings mount to millions. Convert this to trees and one can see how quickly libraries prevent deforestation.

INFORMATION EXPLOSION:
A great deal of online information is neither accurate nor valuable; school librarians teach future generations of information users how to evaluate, make meaning from, and organize into meaning-ful use, the abundance of information with which they are bombarded.

EQUITABLE EDUCATION:
School libraries, by their very nature, provide equitable resources for all students: one library's collection provides equitable information, technology, books and research opportunities for all of the school's children.

FISCALLY MINDED:
The school library is the most cost-effective way to provide resources for all children. Libraries save schools and taxpayers millions of dollars by recycling (i.e., checking out to multiple readers) books, magazines, and other sources of information. See also ENVIRONMENTALISM.

Statewide bidding on electronic resources is an economically sound approach.

CITIZENS' SAFETY:
Cyber-safety saves lives. Teaching critical Internet safety skills, the school librarian helps serve as the school's Cyber Safety-net.

Cyber-bullying, rising faster than any other form of school violence, decreases when schools enforce anti-bullying policies and provide support for the victims of cyber-bullying; libraries can provide safe havens for all those involved.

School libraries offer filtered access to authenticated accurate information.

LIFE-LONG READERS:
Children having access to a large selection of personal-interest reading material gain personal insight and empathy, a broader understanding of the world and his or her place in it, and other important life lessons offered through a strong, well-stocked school library collection.

Fig. 5.3.   Language of political advocacy.   *(continued)*

Schools with strong school library programs "beat the odds." When learning to read becomes reading to learn, school children's reading scores often decline. Children provided greater opportunity for free voluntary reading and selection from material in well-funded school libraries are more likely to beat these odds. (Scholastic 2008).

CHILDREN'S HEALTH:
"Information pollution" limits attention spans of today's school children and can cause health-related issues such as obesity and diabetes. Librarians teach children the art of information synthesizing, a survival skill that allows children to greatly reduce unnecessary online time.
See also CITIZENS' SAFETY.

JOBS OF THE FUTURE:
In 2009, a study of businesses found that employers sought certain skills in new workers (see excerpt from Hart Associates).

HIGH POVERTY:
Children living in poverty are less likely to visit their local library, or have access to technology, information resources, and personal reading material. A well-funded library equitably serves these children's literary and information needs. See also EQUITABLE EDUCATION and DIMINISHING EDUCATION FUNDS.

DIMINISHING EDUCATION FUNDS:
The school library is able to provide the most fiscally-efficient, equitable, yet comprehensive offering of information, resources, and books for children.

STRONG TECHNOLOGY FOCUS:
Librarians teach students how to use social media and Web 2.0 tools as well as ways to effectively and efficiently find accurate information on the Internet.

INTERNATIONAL INTERESTS:
In a global 21st-century information society, efficient and accurate use of information is the power tool of the future. If students wish to continue to compete globally, they must have sophisticated information-seeking tools, research skills taught by the school librarian.

FIRST AMENDMENT RIGHTS:
In multiple cases around the country, many school librarians, armed with the Intellectual Freedom Policy from the American Library Association, have stood up for and offended students, parents, and schools' First Amendments rights.

Fig. 5.3.   *Continued*

unsuccessful at disseminating this research into the mainstream media. Presenting key findings from this research—particularly those results specific to one's own state and relevant to "The Ask"—is imperative to legitimizing the request. While it is important to share the research, legislators do not need to be flooded with these findings. Legislators want a bulleted list with short sentences or phrases similar to sound bites that they can use when needed. If the legislator wants more detail and citations, he or she will ask.

While there are many resources that librarians can provide congresspersons, it is important to recognize that legislators juggle many issues. Thus, providing a one-page only, bulleted handout relevant to "The Ask" is a most important strategy. Figure 5.4 is a list of ideas and resources to aid in creating individual or state-specific legislator packets.

Potential Materials for the Legislator's Packet

One or two-page handouts
- Instructional Role of the School Librarian (what we teach, our curriculum)
- Benefits of a School Library on Academic Achievement
- Status of School Libraries in XYZ State (Maps are quick and easy to read and show impact)
- Regulations or Guidelines on School Libraries in XYZ State
- Inputs Necessary for a Quality School Library Program
- Recommendations or what you are asking for

[Examples of these types of handouts can often be found at state school library websites, such as the Pennsylvania School Librarians Association at http://www.psla.org/index.php/legislation/legislator-your-library-campaign and Washington's School Library Literacy, Information and Technology (LIT) program for 21st Century Learning http://www.k12.wa.us/SchoolLibrary/Standards.aspx.]

Eye-catching booklets, such as:
- *School Libraries Work!* (free from Scholastic and being revised in 2011)
- *Standards for the 21st-Century Learner* (from ALA Bookstore or http://www.ala.org/ala/mgrps/divs/aasl/guidelinesandstandards/learningstandards/standards.cfm)
- Copy of statewide research conducted in many states (refer to School Library Impact Studies Project at http://libweb.mansfield.edu//upload/kachel/ClassChart.pdf to locate references to the various state studies)
- Copy of "School Library Programs Improve Student Learning: Policymakers" (the AASL Advocacy brochure from ALA Bookstore or http://www.ala.org/ala/mgrps/divs/aasl/aaslissues/brochures/advocacybrochures.cfm)
- Any other relevant state or local school library brochures

Fig. 5.4.   Legislator packet materials.

The Legislator Visit

An advocacy campaign cannot successfully affect legislation without ongoing in-person contacts with legislators. The advocacy team should create a short list of three to five library-friendly legislators who they believe will help fulfill their request: to sponsor (or "author") a bill or resolution. Visit legislators in small groups (two to three) and be well polished in the presentation of information as well as the request. Always call to make an appointment with the legislator's scheduler. Requesting a visit in the legislator's local district office is often the best. Legislators are not as distracted or busy as when they are in the capital. It is likely a closer drive for the librarians as well.

However, scheduling an appointment in the capital has an advantage because appointments can be scheduled with most of the legislators on the short list. When the legislator's prior commitments defer a visit, meet with the aide who handles education and library issues. Often meeting with aides provides memorable contacts for follow-up. Aides often have more time and pay particular attention to the issue as they will have to report back to the legislator. Be sure to inform the scheduler who else will be attending the meeting and ask for an e-mail address to send prepared handouts prior to the visit. Follow up the phone call with an e-mail confirmation of the meeting detailing names, titles, addresses, and e-mails of everyone attending. Be sure to state if the librarians are representing a state library organization. Try to include a constituent from the legislator's district; legislators are more concerned about representing the people who vote for them. The scheduler may even ask if the group has constituent representation.

Take a prepared packet of materials to the meeting with extra copies for the legislator's distribution. Be prepared to give and receive business cards. They can be printed inexpensively and show professionalism. Present "The Ask" and why it is needed, or present the problems that need to be resolved, asking the legislator for advice on how to proceed. Understand that in order for the legislator to act on the request, he will need to hear two things: First and foremost, how many constituents support this request? If the group represents a school library association, be sure to mention the number of members. Secondly, what will the group do to increase and rally more support? Whether through LISTSERVs, school library organizations, or blogs, the legislator will need to know that the requesting group or individual librarians can and will organize the support needed to move legislation. It is also helpful if the group offers to meet with other legislators to present the issue to garner more support. The legislator may provide names of other legislators the group should visit. Offer to gather additional information the legislator may need and know that it is appropriate to ask for advice on how to proceed.

Politics is give and take, so after the request has been presented and discussed, offer some publicity opportunities for the legislator. Invite the legislator to a school library in his district to observe these claims, including a photo op and press release, or invite the legislator to speak at an upcoming meeting or conference that the local press will cover. For example, in appreciation of Senator Patty Murray's first senator sponsorship of the SKILLs Act, the Washington Library Media Association (WLMA) Advocacy Committee wasted no time in nominating her for a special Presidential Library Advocacy Award, honoring her at the state conference.

Always follow the visit with a thank you e-mail, card, or letter and appoint a person to follow up with the legislator or his aide. Follow-up is critical, as a one-time visit is likely to produce nothing but goodwill. A common error constituents make is assuming that a one-time contact whether through e-mail, phone call, or a meeting is enough for a legislator to act on. If the team visits other legislators, the appointed contact person should call the legislator or the aide back later to report which legislators were visited and their reactions to the issue. This sends a clear message that the group intends to actively pursue this issue and will continue to contact the legislator. This often prompts action.

The preparation for the legislator visit will certainly outweigh the time you spend in the legislator's office—typically 15 to 20 minutes. If the meeting is longer, the legislator is interested. It may seem intimidating to brief a legislator, but in this case, the librarian is the expert and, on behalf of students, needs to share her or his library expertise. Legislators need to be educated on the basics of school libraries, the research supporting them, and the issues involved in providing equitable and quality library programs to all students. The messages or themes used in these visits need to relate to "The Ask." See figure 5.5 for ideas of broad topics or messages that librarians want legislators to understand; some may be appropriate to include on one-page handouts or as prompts in meetings. (These are meant simply as a starting point; librarians will

Messages that can be used with legislators
- Libraries impact student achievement, first and foremost. By improving the library staffing and resources, student achievement could be improved.
- School librarians are teachers.
- School librarians teach essential information usage skills used in every curriculum and needed to prepare students for college and careers.
- Communities need employees with the problem-solving, analysis, and critical thinking skills that school librarians teach.
- School librarians teach students about cyber-curriculum: cyber-safety, identity protection.
- Librarians teach students internet information skills: how to find, communicate, and ethically reuse information from the Internet.
- School libraries provide access to books and technology to develop readers and a lifelong habit of reading.
- School libraries save money by economically sharing and reusing instructional resources throughout the school.
- The school library program is the one program that impacts every student and teacher, economically managing resource provisions for the whole school.
- There is an abundance of research that shows that students in schools with certificated librarians and good school libraries learn more, get better grades, and score higher on standardized test scores than students in schools without libraries.
- The school library is the learning laboratory of the classroom; it is not a peripheral, add-on service.
- The school librarian is a student advocate for ensuring equitable access to ideas and technologies for all students including those with special learning needs.
- Libraries provide equity—all students and all schools will benefit from this legislation, including special education students and English language learners.

Fig. 5.5. Messages for legislators.

want to provide greater detail according to individual needs.) Convey messages in simple and clear language, free of library jargon.

See figure 5.6 for potential questions legislators may ask; librarians should be prepared with answers that show they are organized, serious, and knowledgeable. Legislators are interested in their own districts or state. Therefore, try to gather some demographic data about school libraries they represent. State school library organizations and state departments of education provide sources for state data. The *School Libraries Count* annual survey data collected by AASL is another good source (http://www.ala.org/ala/mgrps/divs/aasl/researchandstatistics/slcsurvey/slcsurvey.cfm). Members of ALA/AASL can also contact the ALA Washington office and ask to speak to someone in the Office of Government Relations for information (http://www.ala.org/ala/aboutala/offices/wo/index.cfm).

Success Stories as Models of School Library Legislative Advocacy

The Pennsylvania Story

In Pennsylvania during the disastrous state budget cuts of 2009–2010, the Pennsylvania School Librarians Association (PSLA) joined a coalition called the Pennsylvania School Funding Campaign (http://www.paschoolfunding.org). This led to many effective partnerships with other education organizations that included school

What Legislators May Ask About School Libraries:
- What are the school libraries like in my district/state? How many do not have libraries or certified librarians? How does that compare nationally or to other parts of the state?
- Is there research and evidence to support your request?
- Will the library/grassroots organization work to get more support for this issue, including meeting with other legislators?
- Is there a growing group of my constituents who care about this topic? (evidenced by increased e-mails, phone calls, and letters)?
- Is the library/grassroots organization organized and prepared to contact other education and parent organizations to garner more support?
- Who is the appointed library contact person for my office to contact as this issue progresses?
- If students have computers and the Internet, do they really need fully resourced and staffed school libraries?
- Can't the students use the local public libraries?
- Would it be possible to combine the school and public libraries in our area to provide services more economically?
- What would you suggest we cut instead of school libraries if this issue requires funding?

Fig. 5.6.   Questions from legislators.

administrators, parents, teachers, and other student advocacy groups. One such partnership with the Education Law Center of Pennsylvania (ELC) (http://www.elc-pa.org/) has been most productive. As a family and student advocacy nonprofit that primarily represents special education students, the disabled, and English-language learners, ELC (with staff lobbyists, lawyers, and communications experts) helped PSLA work with the Pennsylvania General Assembly to draft and secure passage of a House resolution to complete a comprehensive study of school libraries. Without the advice and guidance of ELC, this would not have happened. The message here is to reach out to other organizations that have different areas of expertise and that can help advance the school library advocacy agenda. This also increases the number of constituents interested in school library issues and, thus, the interest of the legislator to push forward.

The Washington Story

In Washington state, the campaign to garner support for federal legislation that includes school libraries as part of basic education began in earnest in the fall of 2010. Advocates organically evolved from the state's school library organization, the WLMA's Advocacy Committee (WLMAAC). From contacts at ALA's Washington, D.C., office—Kristen Murphy, Jeff Kratz, and Emily Sheketoff—Advocacy Committee members were advised to focus efforts on Senator Patty Murray. Sheketoff's political insight and Murray's personal story and voting record indicated that she would be a likely candidate, although initial contacts to Murray's office indicated school libraries were not on her radar. The work began in earnest to both educate and communicate.

Beginning in fall 2010, WLMAAC made contacts with Murray's office that included expressing appreciation of her work for education, research of her support and voting record, bringing "the message" with regard to 21st-century school libraries, and inviting her to visit a school library.

It was not enough, however, for a few WLMAAC members to be vocal. WLMAAC gathered support from around the state by contacting Washington librarians requesting similar tactics: contacts to Murray's office (appreciation, describing the work of librarians, asking for support) and e-mails inviting her legislative aides to visit.

Not long after, WLMAAC was contacted by Murray's office indicating that she had heard the message because WLMAAC delivered "numbers," that she was interested in working with librarians toward legislation, and that a visit from a legislative aide was in order.

Next, carefully orchestrated arrangements for Murray's legislative aide's visit to the Vancouver Library program were arranged. Important advocacy strategies were implemented: positive appreciation, data on the library's role in student success rates, and showcasing exciting new programs that involved the school library. A second visit followed the introduction of Murray's literacy legislation when WLMAAC saw that this legislation needed increased inclusion of school library.

Shortly after the second legislative aide visit, Senator Murray became the first U.S. senator to sign as sponsor to the SKILLs Act. This was no small feat; it came at a time when Murray became cochair of the 12-member super-committee working with President Obama on fiscal solutions to the catastrophic budget crisis. The story of Senator Murray's cosponsorship of the SKILLs Act stands as one of the strongest examples of legislative advocacy's effectiveness.

In Summary

To build effective legislative advocacy, school librarians must know what is acceptable for political involvement, what is involved in the political process, how to devise "The Ask" in terms requesting action from legislators, which legislators to approach, how to craft the message, and the components of planning a legislative visit.

It is important to realize that school library *legislative* advocacy begins with the development of a relationship between school library advocates and legislative decision makers. Educating oneself about key issues of interest to legislators and, in turn, educating legislators about school libraries through their key issues is the basis for capturing the attention of lawmakers and beginning to build this relationship.

Once the elements of building effective legislative advocacy are understood and the legislator's perspective is identified, the next goal is to provide clear and consistent communication, based on research, establishing the school librarian as an expert who can be trusted and seen as credible.

The power of the school librarian's involvement in legislative advocacy cannot be overlooked or dismissed. School librarians and school libraries need national and state legislative involvement to curb the erosion of school libraries that is taking place throughout the nation. It will take the power of many to create the impact needed to create mandates that support strong school library programs. This will depend on the efforts of individual school librarians and coalitions of advocates who actively work to raise awareness of legislators, resulting in action for school library programs.

References

American Association of School Librarians. *Advocacy*. http://www.ala.org/ala/mgrps/divs/aasl/aaslissues/advocacy/definitions.cfm (accessed November 13, 2011).

Hart Research Associates. *Raising the Bar: Employers' Views on College Learning in the Wake of the Economic Downturn: A Survey among Employers Conducted on Behalf of the Association of American Colleges and Universities.* Hart Research, 2010. http://www.aacu.org/leap/documents/2009_EmployerSurvey.pdf (accessed September 30, 2011).

Kachel, Debra E. "School Library Research Summarized: A Graduate Class Project." Mansfield University, Pennsylvania. *School Library Impact Studies Project.* 2011. http://libweb.mansfield.edu/upload/kachel/ImpactStudy.pdf (accessed September 30, 2011).

Pribesh, Shana, Karen Gavigan, and Gail Dickinson. "The Access Gap: Poverty and Characteristics of School Library Media Centers." *Library Quarterly* 81, no. 2 (April 2011): 143–60.

School Libraries Work! Research Foundation Paper. Scholastic, 2008. http://listbuilder.scholastic.com/content/stores/LibraryStore/pages/images/SLW3.pdf (accessed November 13, 2011).

Vance, Stephanie. "Make the Darn Ask." In "Tipsheet." *Advocacy Guru.* http://advocacyguru.com/resources/tipsheet/#june10 (accessed September 30, 2011).

Additional Resources

American Association of School Librarians. *School Libraries Count.* http://www.ala.org/ala/mgrps/divs/aasl/researchandstatistics/slcsurvey/slcsurvey.cfm (accessed November 13, 2011).

American Association of School Librarians. "School Library Programs Improve Student Learning: Policymakers." AASL Advocacy Brochure. http://www.ala.org/ala/mgrps/divs/aasl/aaslissues/brochures/advocacybrochures.cfm (accessed November 13, 2011).

American Association of School Librarians. *Standards for the 21st-Century Learner.* American Library Association, 2007. http://www.ala.org/aasl/standards (accessed October 7, 2009).

Chen, Diane R. "The Importance of the Library Media Specialist as a Political Voice." *School Library Media Activities Monthly* 23, no. 10 (June 2007): 46–48.

International Society for Technology in Education. "Advocacy-Guided Templates and Starter Kits." *ISTE.* http://www.iste.org/about-iste/advocacy/templates-and-starter-kits.aspx (accessed March 14, 2012).

Kaaland, Christie. "Legislator in the Library Day: A Model for Legislative Advocacy." *School Library Monthly* 26, no. 7 (March 2010): 44–46.

Kaaland, Christie. "School Library Language for Legislators." *School Library Monthly* 27, no. 6 (March 2011): 49–51.

Kachel, Debra E. "Beyond the Library Door: The Story of Pennsylvania's HR 987." *School Library Monthly* 27, no. 7 (April 2011): 49–51.

Kachel, Debra E. "School Library Advocacy-Federal Legislators." *Mansfield University School Library Department LibGuide.* http://libraryschool.campusguides.com/aecontent.php?pid=244879&sid=2074779 (accessed October 1, 2011).

Kachel, Debra E. *School Library Impact Studies Chart.* "School Library Research Summarized: A Graduate Class Project." Mansfield University, Pennsylvania. http://libweb.mansfield.edu//upload/kachel/ClassChart.pdf (accessed September 30, 2011).

Krashen, Stephen. *The Power of Reading.* Portsmouth, N.H.: Heinemann, 2004.

Levitov, Deborah. "Language—Communication or Jargon?" *School Library Media Activities Monthly* 24, no. 5 (January 2008): 45–46.

Library Advocates Handbook. Rev. ed. Washington, D.C.: American Library Association, 2006. http://www.ala.org/ala/aboutala/offices/ola/libraryadvocateshandbook.cfm (accessed October 1, 2011).

Longley, Robert. "Letters to Congress" *About.com Guide.* http://usgovinfo.about.com/od/uscongress/a/letterscongress.htm (accessed November 13, 2011).

McGhee, Marla. "Having a School Library Work Plan." *School Library Monthly* 28, no. 6 (March 2012): 32–34.

Ray, Mark. "Big Picture Advocacy: Making Fifteen Minutes Count." *School Library Monthly* 28, no. 6 (March 2012): 29–31.

Rogers, Curtis, Kristin Murphy, and Stephanie Vance. "Libraries, Advocacy and Social Media." *Vimeo.com.* http://vimeo.com/7347082 (accessed October 1, 2011).

Schuckett, Sandy. *Political Advocacy for School Librarians: You Have the Power!* Worthington, Ohio: Linworth, 2004.

Sheketoff, Emily. "Federal Legislative Action: Key to Your Library Media Center's Success." *School Library Media Activities Monthly* 23, no. 4 (December 2006): 50–51.

Vance, Stephanie. *Citizens in Action: A Guide to Influencing Government.* Bethesda, Md.: Columbia Books, 2009.

Vance, Stephanie D. "Effective Advocacy Checklist." *Advocacy Guru.* http://advocacyguru.com/resources/effective-advocacy-checklist/ (accessed October 1, 2011).

Vance, Stephanie D. *Government by the People: How to Communicate with Congress.* Washington, D.C.: Advocacy Associates, 1999.

Vance, Stephanie D. "Make the Darn Ask" (free podcast). *iTunes.* http://www.apple.com/itunes/podcasts/fanfaq.html (accessed September 30, 2011).

Online Resources

American Library Association (ALA). Legislative Action Center. http://capwiz.com/ala/home/

American Library Association. ALA Washington office. http://www.ala.org/ala/aboutala/offices/wo/index.cfm

Pennsylvania School Librarians Association. *Legislator @ Your Library Campaign.* http://www.psla.org/index.php/legislation/legislator-your-library-campaign

State of Washington Office of Superintendent of Public Instruction. *School Library Media Programs and Teacher-Librarians: State Learning Standards.* http://www.k12.wa.us/SchoolLibrary/Standards.aspx

6

Working with Parents, Community Groups, and Businesses

Sarah Applegate, David Schuster, and Roz Thompson

The local and regional community plays an important role in understanding and supporting school libraries. There are many ways in which school librarians can work with parents, community members, and local businesses to promote reading and literacy activities, and to motivate and engage students in learning. Establishing key relationships with these groups serves to raise their awareness about school libraries, which can lead to advocacy support via these audiences. As a result, these relationships can also help ensure the continuation of vibrant school library programs that support student learning.

Community

In the local and regional communities, there are several different types of groups that can partner with school libraries to lend support and strengthen the learning experiences of students. These include:

- Public Libraries
- College or University Libraries and Students
- Community Groups (nonprofits)
- City Governments and Businesses
- Parents

Working with Public Libraries

A natural connection for school librarians to make is with the staff at the local public library. During the school year, students have the benefit of using both their school library space and their public library space to get information, to study, and to access online resources. A strong school library program will work with the local community library to ensure that once the school year ends, students can continue getting Internet access, reading materials, and adult help from the public library. The school librarian has a responsibility to communicate with the public library staff about the information needs of the student body, so that the public librarians can work to maintain an active level of student engagement about ideas and information throughout the summer months. Cultivating this relationship will not only help students but also create interest and support within the ecosystem of libraries.

In addition to providing materials and a physical place to hang out, public librarians can work with the school librarian throughout the year on many different programs to engage and encourage learning. Keep in mind that these activities can go both ways: School librarians can participate in a community library program and/or invite community librarians to participate in school library programs. Here is a list of ideas followed with a brief description.

Summer Reading Programs

Many communities have a summer reading program that is advertised through the school library program. Community librarians will visit schools in the spring and explain the program and activities to students. They hope to sign up students to participate or volunteer as needed. Working with community librarians on a joint summer reading program may also help students because school librarians know which books may enhance student learning the following school year.

Teen Advisers and Volunteers

Public librarians often will advertise for their youth programs through the school librarian and hope to have several middle or high school students serve on their advisory board or serve as volunteers. School librarians can recommend avid readers or interested students to the public librarians, and these students can play a valuable role in helping their community library with program ideas for teens as well as create connections between school and public libraries.

Teen Book Groups

Public libraries often sponsor teen book groups where students talk about books that interest them, play games, do crafts, and eat food together. Many times, these are activities that school librarians have difficulty finding time to do during the school day or there isn't extra money available for some of these activities. Here again is another opportunity for students to spend time with friends talking about books and ideas that are interesting to them, and school librarians can join these groups on occasion. These groups are very effective at developing lifelong public library users and advocates.

Public Library Cards and Student Public Library Use

School librarians should encourage their students to acquire a public library card so that the students can take advantage of all the resources available to them. Besides using library cards to check out books, it also gives them access to many valuable online resources such as subscription databases that the public library has purchased and that may not be available to the local school district. Students should be encouraged to use this access regularly, even during the school day, to help with research. School librarians should take an active role in teaching students how to use the Web site and Web resources throughout the year.

Public librarians are excited and supportive of students getting library cards and using online public library databases. Have a stack of applications at your school library, offer to deliver completed applications and pick up completed cards, promising "never leave school" delivery. Make sure your library has an "institutional card" so that when you are instructing students on public library online resources, they can still have access with a school-specific card. Public libraries typically have access to many more databases and tools than school libraries do. A great way to provide additional resources to students (without affecting your school budget!) is to work with the public library to get students trained on the databases at the public library so that they can use the resources at school and home. Be sure to keep running statistics of how many students were assisted in getting public library cards and be sure to point out the important learning resources gained by the student when reporting the statistics.

Visiting Authors

When authors come to visit community libraries and local bookstores, school librarians can often piggyback on these visits and help with advertising and drumming up interest in reading books by the author. School librarians can purchase additional copies of books, give book talks to classes, and create displays in the school library. School librarians can also provide student volunteers to help with the public events, if needed. If school libraries are lucky enough to have visiting authors, be sure to invite the local public librarians to these events so that more community people have the benefit of sharing in the fun.

Adult Book Club

A school librarian may lead book groups with his teaching staff. One group of people to reach out to is public librarians as they, too, are interested in educational or topical issues that can be covered in the books chosen to be read. Working together in this collaborative manner is not only valuable for sharing ideas but fun as well. The focus on building relationships between key members in an educational community helps to strengthen the experience that students have in the community with their libraries while establishing connections that can become important for school library advocacy efforts over time.

Data and Dessert Night

This idea involves inviting the public librarian to come to the local high school on an evening in late spring. Invite the incoming ninth graders and their parents to come visit the high school library to learn about resources that are offered there and at the local library through presentations by the school and public librarian. Many times, local libraries have many more resources (such as online databases) that are accessible for students with the use of their library card. This united front shows parents in the community that there is a coordinated effort to help students be successful in school. Be sure to bring cookies and punch!

Spring Honors Read and Essay Contest

Many schools require all of their students to read the same book. At one school in Washington state, students in 9th- to 12th-grade honors English/Advanced Placement (AP) classes read the same book each spring after AP testing is over. These books are usually contemporary nonfiction books, and lessons integrating other subjects such as science and art take place. The local library helps support this event by being involved in the adult book club discussion for the book and participating in any community events that may be planned. In addition, the Friends of the Library annually awards $100 to the winners of the student essay contest on a topic related to the book. The school librarian collects the essays and the public librarian (and a group of others) chooses the top three essays. Gifts cards to local stores are awarded to these students.

College University Library and Students

Working with Postsecondary Institution Libraries

The next step for many high school students is a postsecondary institution, whether that is a community college, trade or technical school, or a university. It is helpful for school librarians to meet with the library staff at this next level to gain an understanding of what kind of information literacy skills students need to have. Set up an appointment with one or more of these librarians and have a list of questions to ask. Be prepared to share what goes on at the school library with the college and university librarians.

Another idea is to have students take a field trip to a local college or university library to see how it differs from their school or to enhance their research on a school project. Through colleges and universities, field trip opportunities can be organized to take advantage of programs in place at these institutions, such as an organic farming community, an art program, a museum, or a science fair. Knowing people in these educational communities can be very advantageous to setting up this experience for students in grades K–12.

Finally, school library associations may have contacts with college and university programs that will allow them to use their facilities such as meeting rooms and computer labs for a nominal fee. This can help defray the costs for board meetings or training and helps maintain a link between school and college librarians. This connection has helped contain meeting costs for the Washington Library Media Association while developing positive relationships with universities.

Working with University Students

Students in local colleges and universities are potential advocates for school library programs. School librarians can provide support and education for new and potential teachers. One idea is to host students who need to earn community service hours or are potential education majors. They not only will get their hours, but they will also find out the possibilities and potential of school libraries. Another idea is to do presentations to local teacher education programs. Most teacher education programs provide very little information about what school librarians and school library programs do for students and teachers. Reaching out to future teachers allows for school librarians to shape the message about school libraries, create potential advocates, and help future teachers understand the role, responsibilities, and opportunities for working with school librarians.

Working with Community Groups and Businesses

Nonprofits

Many school-age students are expected or required to participate in community service projects. The school librarian can sometimes be a liaison to these groups to help students get involved with projects. At a high school in Washington state, the school librarian works with the English teachers to plan a special field trip each spring after the honors/AP English students finish reading a common nonfiction book. On some of the past field trips, students have performed community service for groups such as Habitat for Humanity, the South Sound Reading Foundation, and Room to Read.

In addition, because many community groups (e.g., churches, Girl and Boy Scouts, parent groups, reunion committees) may use the school library as a meeting space in the evenings or on weekends, school librarians develop a relationship with people in their communities. These are important relationships to maintain and cultivate since they can lead to discussions about the role of school librarians and how important they are in the educational process.

City Governments

While it doesn't seem like a logical or easy connection for school libraries to work with city governments, from an advocacy point of view it could be a powerful and worthwhile connection to develop. For example, one school district in Lacey, Washington, has developed a "One City, One Book" project that is a collaboration between the school district, the city government, a local nonprofit, and the public library. This powerful partnership has created a long-term, positive, interdependent relationship among these different players, resulting in an expectation in the community for this annual event to occur. Each year, a feature author is selected and students from around the district read and celebrate that author's writing. The project culminates with the author presenting at a public venue in addition to presenting for students. The city has participated by proclaiming February as "Lacey Loves to Read Month" and providing a space for the author to speak. The city has also provided promotional materials and published information in its newsletters and on its Web site, reaching a wide audience. The city also publishes "Lacey Loves to Read" announcements on water bills and puts out electronic billboards (typically used for construction projects) announcing the author event. Some years, they have even had reading groups in city offices and promotional events at city council meetings.

Working with Businesses

School librarians have many opportunities to establish relationships with businesses. In each of these relationships, it helps library advocacy to talk about opportunities and challenges that school libraries currently face. It is important to educate many different audiences about the state of education and the importance of a well-staffed and well-maintained library and how it will positively affect student learning. Some of the key partnerships for school librarians include working with people employed at places like these:

- Local bookstores
- National bookstores
- Grocery stores
- Craft stores
- Restaurants
- Parents' places of employment
- Other vendors related to libraries or schools

There is a wide variety of ways that school librarians can connect with these potential business partners. A beginning step would be mentioning your work when you make a purchase. Striking up a conversation about your school library program and the role of student research in student learning helps educate business owners about the "new face" of school libraries as active, exciting, and busy learning spaces. A next step may be asking for donations for a library event, an award, or gifts for library volunteers. The Washington Library Media Association connects with vendors by asking for donations for the annual Legislative Auction. Businesses and vendors work hard to have positive images in the community, and contributing money and goods to school libraries is one way to show their support for students in their community. Be sure to publish the names of businesses that support your projects and send grateful thank you notes. All arrangements should consider how to make the partnership *a give-and-take arrangement that can be advantageous for both.*

Grants from Businesses

Local businesses are often very interested in finding high-profile ways of supporting schools. A teacher-librarian can be the coordinator of these grants by reaching out and making connections with businesses. If a teacher is interested in going on a field trip to a local museum, for example, a local business might be willing to provide funds for buses and then provide a space for post–field trip art projects to be displayed in the business. A specific type of business might also be interested in supporting a curricular project or topic that is connected to its business; for example, a company involved in alternative energy might be willing to support a classroom project around alternative energy or providing funds for specific print or video materials about the topic. School librarians have wide informational expertise and access to human and online resources, which enables them to be available to help teachers plan special activities. Inevitably, these collaborative efforts create advocates and supporters of our roles and positions in education.

Working with Parents

Leadership takes on several different forms, and it is up to the librarian to take the initiative to establish relationships and connections. What this means generally is that librarians need to step out of their comfort zone and find others who have similar interests and draw them into the library. Parent organizations such as the Parent Teacher

Association (PTA) are a natural source of collaboration for the school library since parents have a high interest in supporting the school and the students in the learning environment.

Find the following resource in the appendix on page 110: "Use This Page: Creating a Parent Advocacy Plan," *School Library Media Activities Monthly* 23, no. 6 (February 2007). This page provides a guide for developing a school library advocacy plan for parents using a template for planning. Additional resources are listed.

The school librarian can examine the program and identify what is needed to make improvements. Then the parent program (such as the PTA) can be approached as a collaborator to successfully reach certain goals. Everything done needs to focus on students; collaborations can be one-time initiatives or ongoing. After the first collaboration, large or small, awareness of the library is heightened for parents within the school community.

Collaborative Example

Here is one example of a successful collaboration between the Texas Parent Teacher Association (TxPTA) and the Texas Association of School Librarians (TASL). This unique partnership created multiple opportunities to promote the school library through the establishment of an award by the state library association. For the award, the campus PTAs throughout the state and the librarian nominate their campus for a successful project/collaboration. The library association evaluates the collaboration and recommends the winner and then presents the award. To further capitalize on the award, a booth or table along with a presentation might be placed on the agenda at other conferences or meetings, focusing on the value of school libraries. In addition, articles could be written to highlight the role of the school library to parents based on the award.

The concept of the award was conceived when the executive directors of both state organizations were attending an executive directors' conference and talking about challenges faced by both associations. Pairing their strengths and goals made sense for this collaboration. Both of these groups have executive directors, and TASL has a board willing to work with the TxPTA board. Both organizations focus on students, reading, and advocacy throughout the state. The Texas PTA has 30 board members from across the state, and they draw their membership from the leadership from individual districts, each of which has own "council" at the district level. Each person/family becomes a member of the local PTA and a member of the state organization, which equals over 600,000 members overall.

TASL began the award project by building a resource kit (see the Texas Library Association Web site (http://www.txla.org/tasl/parent-resources). The materials are organized into two sections and all the information is freely available for use without further permission.

Section I: Working with Parents: Materials for Parents

Parents are powerful allies and this section shows strategies that can be used to educate parents about the role of librarian in schools. It demonstrates the impact of the school library on a child's learning. It also emphasizes to parents the importance of reading to children and defining information literacy skills. The documents are available in both English and Spanish on the Web site. This section includes:

1. Check sheet with tips for librarians
2. Introduction to parents
3. Twenty-first-century skills article, which focuses on the American Association of School Librarians (AASL) standards and the importance of skills for success learning and living
4. Review of reading lists sponsored by the state that are freely available to parents
5. Links to the AASL Web site: How School Librarians Can Assist You in Reading with Your Children and the importance of reading aloud to children (http://www.ala.org/aasl/aboutaasl/aaslcommunity/quicklinks/el/elread)
6. *School Libraries Work* (Scholastic 2008): Why Care about School Libraries

Section II: Working with PTAs

1. Check sheet on ways to work with the PTA in developing relationships, offering programs, and educating parents about the importance of school libraries
2. Copy of a resolution to support school library programs
3. Letter to the PTA president from the librarian
4. Suggested calendar of events
5. Overview and checklist for two special program opportunities: Healthy Lifestyles and a Technology Fair involving the library; the PTA provides resources and an outline for planning and presenting the events
6. List of library volunteer opportunities

PowerPoint: "Short Introduction to the School Library"

It's Not Just Books and Stories! A Look at School Library Standards (Texas Standards accessed through the Texas State Library and Archives): A 23–30-minute presentation including what a successful school library program looks like, including research done by Texas, Alaska, Colorado, and Pennsylvania studies with an extensive list of works cited.

This toolkit was designed so that building librarians or an association could take the documents and edit them for their individual needs. A webinar introduced this information and provided interaction between librarians and parents.

The award recognizes an outstanding collaboration between a PTA organization and school library. Projects and efforts at both the local campus and district levels are eligible.

Criteria Used for Evaluating Applications

• Purpose/objectives
• Descriptions of program/service
• Results of programs/service
• Extent of collaboration
• Extent of improvement to education and/or advance literacy

Award-Winning Examples

Home/School Reading Program

When PTAs and school libraries work together to promote reading, the benefits provide lasting results. The "Home/School Reading Program" is a program that encourages students to consistently read at home to improve reading skills and to read for pleasure. The program connects parents with the school, working with teachers to promote reading.

Each year, the PTA and librarian choose a theme. Commitment letters are sent home requiring the parent's signatures. K–2 students read at home for a minimum of 60 minutes weekly, third-graders to fifth-graders read at home for a minimum of 80 minutes weekly. Calendars distributed to students are returned every Friday. PTA members tabulate students' reading minutes. Weekly prizes provided by the PTA are given to students who meet their goal. Banners, handmade by the PTA, are hung over classroom doors for classes that meet their group goal. Reading Buddies, which are PTA members and community volunteers, are assigned to children needing help reaching weekly goals.

In addition, the library has a special reading area that is decorated according to the Home/School Reading theme. The PTA members work during the summer to build a reading space in the library. Different themes used throughout the years have included the following: "Revved Up for Reading," "Launch into Literacy," "Cuddle Up with a Bear-y Good Book," "Chill Out with a Good Book!"

Because of a strong PTA and library connection along with the commitment to help each child succeed, the PTA pays to keep the library open for six weeks in the summer. The library is staffed by a certified school librarian and four certified teachers who tutor students needing extra help in reading and math. The library is also opened for the whole community. Students who attend regularly receive a free book at the end of the summer session.

What are the results? Students who are eager readers, parents committed to read with their children, and a PTA that provides 25 weekly volunteers and untold volunteer hours to support the library, a feeling of connection between families and the school, along with students who love to read!

Family Literacy Night

Another very doable example of a successful collaboration is a family literacy night. The PTA partnered with the school library to organize and facilitate a family literacy night called Campus Reads. There were 16 literacy stations developed for the event. The school had not previously hosted a literacy night, and educating parents about literacy opportunities would greatly benefit the families of the school. Many of the stations included technology, such as recorded books, student book trailers, and guest-favorite downloadable books for families to enjoy at the click of a mouse. Several members of the PTA along with the library staff planned the event, which included:

- Reading therapy dogs—students could read to the dogs
- Buddy reading—younger students could read to fifth-grade library assistants and receive a book
- Book swap—students bring in gently used books and trade for another

- Bookmark making
- Downloadables—encouraged students to bring iPods and library cards to learn how to download audio books from the public library
- E-books—demonstrated different e-books available
- Read with Fancy Nancy
- Story time with Dr. Seuss
- Photo opportunity with Clifford the Big Red Dog
- Meet and greet author—Marjorie Hodgson
- Puppets
- Word Games—Scrabble Slam, Boggle, word searches, crosswords, Mad-Libs, and much more
- Listening stations
- Story wall—added words to an ongoing story on the story wall
- Book trailers—view student-made book trailers and learn to make your own
- Book walk—like a cake walk but for books

The event followed the regular PTA meeting. Each student along with parents visited as many of the 16 stations as possible in an hour and a half. The literacy stations were staffed with parents and teacher volunteers. Each student had a program menu form stamped as he or she completed each station. Forms were collected for a drawing held the next school day. Twenty students won gift certificates to the spring Book Fair.

In this collaboration, the PTA helps to plan and facilitate. They also donate gift certificates for the drawing and purchase books given as prizes in two of the stations.

The results of this collaboration had an impact on over 200 students, along with their parents and siblings, making it one of the best-attended events of the year. In this instance, almost one-third of the school population attended the evening program, meeting the goal of raising awareness of family literacy. Several parents were reminded of games that they could play at home and of ways to make reading and retelling stories more exciting at home. Several students now read to their pets at home after reading with the therapy dogs at Campus Reads. The older students seemed especially excited about the downloadable books and e-books that are available to them on their iPods and iPhones.

In Summary

School librarians have valuable skills and expertise that can not only benefit student learning but benefit the development of strong school library programs. Having a "big picture" of education places the school librarian in a unique and powerful position to help students develop and feed their curiosity, create projects that are meaningful, and provide ways to communicate their learning with others effectively. This can be made even more meaningful when links are made to real-world opportunities by capitalizing on possibilities for partnerships that extend the school experience into the community and the homes of students.

As school librarians work to develop partnerships with parents, community, and businesses through special projects, funding, and events, the potential for learning connections and experiences for students will flourish, and understanding by parents of the role of the school library and school librarian will be expanded. Also, firsthand knowledge and understanding of the school library program will be strengthened with each of these connections. The partnerships developed will provide avenues for identifying, developing, and establishing informed advocates that result in voices of support for the school library.

References

"Use This Page: Creating a Parent Advocacy Plan." *School Library Media Activities Monthly* 23, no. 6 (February 2007): 2.

Additional Resources

American Association of School Librarians. "VII. Outreach." In *Empowering Learners: Guidelines for School Library Media Programs*, 41. Chicago, Ill.: American Library Association, 2009.

Brodie, Carolyn S. "The INFOhio Parent Project: Models to Use." *School Library Media Activities Monthly* 23, no. 6 (February 2007): 49–50.

Byers, Catherine M. "Collective Action @ Your Library." *School Library Media Activities Monthly* 23, no. 5 (January 2007): 48–50.

Byers, Catherine M. "Enlist the Choir." *School Library Media Activities Monthly* 22, no. 2 (October 2005): 47–48.

Byers, Catherine M. "Parent Partnership Power." *School Library Media Activities Monthly* 22, no. 6 (February 2006): 47–48.

DelGuidice, Margaux. "Are You Overlooking a Valuable Resource? A Practical Guide to Collaborating with Your Greatest Ally: The Public Library." *Library Media Connection* 27, no. 6 (May/June 2009): 38–39.

Dias-Mitchell, Laurie. "A Harmonic Convergence in the School Library." *Teacher Librarian* 38, no. 1 (October 2010): 32–33.

Foote, Carolyn. "Everyday Advocacy." *School Library Journal* 56, no. 8 (August 2010): 28–30.

Freda, Cecilia. "Promoting Your Library Program: Getting the Message Out." *Knowledge Quest* 36, no. 1 (September/October 2007): 48–51.

Harvey, Carl A. "Connecting the Library Media Center and Parents." *School Library Media Activities Monthly* 23, no. 6 (February 2007): 25–27.

Harvey, Carl A. "Looking from All Perspectives." *School Library Media Activities Monthly* 22, no. 3 (November 2005): 44–47.

Levitov, Deborah D. "Parents: Powerful Advocates." *School Library Media Activities Monthly* 23, no. 6 (February 2007): 4.

Milam, Peggy Creighton. "Impact as a 21st-Century Library Media Specialist." *School Library Media Activities Monthly* 24, no. 7 (March 2008): 39–43.

Milam, Peggy Creighton. "Platinum Partners." *School Library Media Activities Monthly* 24, no. 8 (April 2008): 50–52.

Preddy, Leslie. "Literacy Committee: Creating a Community of Readers." *School Library Monthly* 26, no. 1 (September 2009): 43–47.

Resh, Shannon, Roberta Greene, and George Matthew. "Making Connections @ the Library: Celebrating Collaborations between the School and the Public Library." *Learning & Media* 37, no. 3 (Summer 2009): 5–6.

Ritzo, Christopher, Chaebong Nam, and Bertram Bruce. "Building a Strong Web: Connecting Information Spaces in Schools and Communities." *Library Trends* 58, no. 1 (Summer 2009): 82–94.

School Libraries Work! Research Foundation Paper. Scholastic, 2008. http://listbuilder.scholastic
.com/content/stores/LibraryStore/pages/images/SLW3.pdf (accessed November 13,
2011).

Schuckett, Sandy. "It Takes a Village." *School Library Media Activities Monthly* 23, no. 2 (October
2006): 48–51.

Staino, Rocco. "Friends Groups: Finding Their Way into Library Media Centers." *School Library
Media Activities Monthly* 24, no. 3 (November 2007): 43–45.

Vincelette, Pete, and Priscilla Queen. "School and Public Library Collaboration." *School Library
Monthly* 28, no. 4 (January 2012): 14–16.

Whelan, Debra. "Website Helps School Libraries Find Donors." *School Library Journal* 57, no. 1
(January 2011): 17.

7

Building Champions in the School Community

Debra E. Kachel, Margaux DelGuidice, and Rose Luna

"Now all we need is a champion," states the White Queen when faced with fighting the Jabberwocky to redeem her fallen country.

—Tim Burton's film version of *Alice in Wonderland*

Why Isn't the Voice of the Librarian Enough?

No one will argue the point that the building librarian is the most informed person to advocate for the school library program. The school librarian, after all, has spent years training for the position, and understands the curriculum and information needs of students and teachers, the budget and resources required to support those needs, how to integrate information and technology use skills with classroom content, and how to use evidence-based practices to justify and align the school library program within the overall mission of the school. However, advocacy is not an individual endeavor. It requires working with others to:

- Create a common agenda with school and education decision makers
- Craft and market messages that meet both the library's and other stakeholders' needs
- Lobby effectively in different social and political networks
- Build enduring and supportive partnerships
- Develop a few good champions who represent voices outside the library profession and who will speak up for libraries

Why isn't the voice of the librarian enough? In schools, problems get attention and libraries seldom are perceived as problems. Generally, there is only one librarian in the building, which often promotes isolation. Librarians seamlessly help teachers teach and provide learning resources, sometimes making the teacher look good and receiving far too little credit for their work. In addition, librarians are seldom in the "seat of power," usually by choice or inaction. The "Invisible School Librarian," as often referred to in the library literature, exists in part due to ignorance and a failure to communicate (Hartzell 1997; LaRue 2010; Wilson and MacNeil 1998). This image is often self-created and self-perpetuated because some librarians accept the role of the school library as peripheral rather than integral, maintain the position of isolation instead of inclusion, and do not consider the school library program's mission critical in the academic success of students.

What's It Going to Take?

Becoming influential in a school takes time, hard work, tons of patience and people skills, and a fervent desire to lead and improve a situation. Librarians tend to be reserved, pensive, and willing to watch and be agreeable participants. This is a generalization; however, for Deb Kachel, results from teaching over 10 years at Mansfield showed that 90 percent of the graduate students who completed a Kiersey Temperament Sorter in the School Library Advocacy course were classified as "Guardians" ("Portrait of the Guardian"). Guardians are described as being serious about their duties and responsibilities, dependable and trustworthy, believe in law and order, and respect the rights of others. They are "not very comfortable blazing new trails" but instead work steadily within the system, valuing loyalty, discipline, and teamwork to get the job done right. Guardians are meticulous about schedules and have a sharp eye for proper procedures. Sound familiar?

Clearly, school librarians need to help themselves and help others understand the necessity of school library programs in education. In helping themselves, librarians need to embrace new—and maybe some uncomfortable—dispositions in the areas of leadership and advocacy. A 2009 study, "Exploration to Identify Professional Dispositions of School Librarians: A Delphi Study," identifies dispositions as outwardly manifested, observable behaviors, not personality traits (Bush and Jones 2011, 55); see figure 7.1.

In comparing the Guardian traits to the dispositions above, Guardian librarians have the skill sets, they just need three "Ps"—a push, a plan, and some people. There is no stronger "push" or incentive than losing one's job, and the entire school library profession is at risk. With very few states requiring school librarians or even library programs, dwindling state and local funds to support them, and misguided administrators and policy makers who believe that the Internet can replace a library, there is no time like the present to wear the cloak of leadership and advocacy dispositions and get to work!

Librarians will often justify inaction by stating, "I can't do those things, that's not my personality." Dispositions are not personality traits. Think of them as a mantle of attitudes and behaviors that can be assumed in specific situations as needed. A librar-

Category	Description
Leading/To Lead/ Leadership	moves vision forward, lead by modeling, visionary activist, perseverance, integrity, passion, reflective, honesty, innovator, change agent, risk-taking leader, resilient, move library to center of learning, mentor
Advocacy/ Advocate	communication, positive, inherently optimistic, motivator, leading cheerleader, promotes, uses avenues that yield best results, encourages individual pursuits, creates coalitions, maintenance of relationships

Fig. 7.1.   Described dispositions: Observable behaviors.

ian who is timid, uncertain, or unsure can think of this as an alter ego, like Superman or Wonder Woman. Assume the new identity, try it out, and forge ahead. When the school librarian wears this cloak or mantle of behaviors often enough, the new skills become natural habits (or dispositions).

In developing the advocacy plan, which is more thoroughly discussed in chapter 4, school librarians need to help others from outside the library profession to understand the importance of quality school library programs. School librarians need to build champions who will not just offer support but also actively speak up and argue on behalf of the library program. Voices of others resonate with their member groups and organizations and can accrue support more easily than the voice of the librarian. This is simply human nature. Colleagues generally believe one another since they have a similar set of understandings and beliefs. For example, if a parent library volunteer tells the PTA association that the school librarian is really trying to reach out to English-language learners by developing a Spanish collection and needs financial support, the other PTA members are likely to believe her. If librarians are the only vocal advocates with no outside champions, the message is perceived to be self-serving, sometimes job-protecting, and potentially biased.

Identifying Leaders in Stakeholder Groups

School librarians need to identify stakeholders (those people or groups who have a vested interest in the success of the school library program) as potential library champions, allies, and advocates. Stakeholders can be divided into two basic groups: school (those who work inside the school) and community (those who work outside the school); see figure 7.2. This chapter focuses on the primary school stakeholders identified as teachers, administrators, and school board members. However, there are many stakeholders who can be influential advocates of quality school library programs.

Whether a school librarian has worked in a certain building for many years or has been recently hired, that person needs to assess the work environment to identify the

SCHOOL LIBRARY STAKEHOLDER GROUPS

SCHOOL	COMMUNITY
Teachers	Parents
Students	Taxpayers
Principals	Local business leaders
Other district and area school librarians	Community organizations
District Administrators	Public librarians
Superintendent	Local university faculty and librarians
Technology Coordinators	Museums and other local educational organizations
Curriculum Coordinators	State education and library associations
Department chairpersons/supervisors	State children and youth advocacy organizations
School board members	National education and library organizations
	Legislators and other policy makers

Another good list of stakeholders is identified in the "AASL Crisis Toolkit." http://www.ala.org/ala/mgrps/divs/aasl/aaslissues/toolkits/crisis.cfm

Fig. 7.2.   School library stakeholder groups.

school stakeholder groups and determine the focus of advocacy strategies. A successful advocacy plan will identify the "movers and shakers" within the stakeholder groups—those whom others listen to and follow (whether they have the title or not). These individuals may not be the obvious ones. Normally, one would think that the principal would be the main leader in the school stakeholder group. However, a weak principal who often defers to the building's computer coordinator or lead English teacher might not be the best target for influencing. In this case, focusing advocacy strategies on the computer coordinator or lead English teacher makes more sense.

Conducting an environmental scan to learn the hot topics of concern in the building (not just the library issues) and what others expect from the school library program is another initial step. Assessing the environment can be done via online, anonymous surveys, small focus groups over lunch, or a meeting set up with the principal. Topics will be different for each school and may include an unsettled union contract, a lack of adequate planning time for teachers, a building renovation, a rapidly increasing student population, poor test scores, and so forth. The library program is not an island; all these environmental issues will affect the school library advocacy plan and its success. Gary Hartzell's book *Building Influence for the School Librarian* has some excellent ideas on how to assess the school work environment.

The school librarian may learn that expectations are low for school library services and the teachers, for example, really only want a study hall or babysitting service while they have their planning time. In this case, the choice would be to educate the stakeholders (teachers and principal) about what collaborative instruction and integration of resources can do for student learning and begin to lay out a plan to achieve this goal.

According to *Empowering Learners: Guidelines for School Librarians*, school librarians in their role as advocates must begin with a vision and plan for the school library program that is matched with the needs and priorities of stakeholders (AASL 2009, 42). Therefore, when developing an action advocacy plan, learning what stakeholders want and expect from the school library is as important as knowing what the school library program can deliver.

The Message

After identifying leaders of the school stakeholder groups and figuring out what they are interested in or concerned about, the school librarian needs to craft a message that will hook these stakeholder-leaders. The message may vary slightly from group to group, but the basic message should be clear and straightforward with as little library jargon as possible. The message must focus on students and improving student learning, not the librarian and his or her working conditions. For example, if a school librarian wants a bigger library, support is not likely if that is how the message is presented. Instead, the presentation of the issue should be, "Students need space for small group work, quiet individual study, large class instruction, and computers and production equipment to complete class projects in the library," which will result in general understanding and support. The message must be focused on the student and student learning, not the librarian.

Stakeholders want to know "what's in it for me," easily remembered by "WII-FM," an acronym for an FM radio station. Stakeholders have to see the connection to themselves, their jobs, or their children before they will invest time and effort to become library champions. The savvy school librarian will figure out what the stakeholder values and wants and incorporate those requirements into the action advocacy plan.

Communication with stakeholders needs to be frequent and meaningful. It is critical for the librarian to connect student learning with what is happening in the library and with library resources. No one else really knows the scope of library work, how it is embedded in all curriculum areas, and how it affects student learning, so the librarian must be proactive in communicating. Communications need to be two way: *pushed out*, telling stakeholders about the school library program (public relations), and *pulled in*, communicating with the stakeholder (marketing). Marketing messages appeal to the stakeholders and what is important to them by advertising or providing a service they want or are interested in. For example, promoting a parent page on the library Web site that recommends books for parents to read to kindergartners is a winning marketing strategy.

There are numerous opportunities to communicate through the school and library Web site (include short YouTube videos and Jing-recorded tutorials), parent newsletters, regular library reports, short instructional brochures, an e-mail distribution list (which librarians should continually build), and local media outlets, such as newspapers and television stations. Search the Internet for publications you can adapt. For example, the School Library Link newsletter (http://www.theschoollibrarylink.com/) is a prewritten parent newsletter available free to school librarians to download, print to send home with their students, or link on the library's Web site. (See the appendix, page 111, for "Use This Page: Tips on Using *The School Library Link* in Your School" from *School Library Monthly*, November 2009.)

Building Champions among Teachers

It is interesting that not much has been written to date about building advocates among teachers. It is somewhat assumed that if school librarians effectively collaborate with teachers in helping to teach their subject content while infusing information and technology skills, the teachers will naturally become advocates of the school library program. Although this may be true in most cases, it still does not mean that those teachers are willing to be *active* advocates when needed. Sadly, in today's cost-cutting and staff-reducing economic environment, teachers are unlikely to stand up for school library staff positions when they fear their own jobs might be cut.

However, in crafting the advocacy message, librarians are uniquely qualified to help teachers in many of the areas they care about. Determine the most pressing need and make it a focal point in the teacher champion building advocacy plan. Some examples follow.

Example 1

- TEACHERS care about quality instruction (lesson plans that work).

- LIBRARIAN'S Message
  Teachers and librarians are expert teachers. Teachers provide expertise about curriculum and students. Librarians provide expertise on resources and technology. Together we make a powerful instructional team.

- ACTION ADVOCACY PLAN
  The librarian creates a teacher resource page on the library Web site with links to sample rubrics, lesson-plan generators, and standards. She also creates a database of previously implemented, collaboratively taught units for all teachers to modify and reuse.

Example 2

- TEACHERS care about helping English-language learners in their classes.

- LIBRARIAN'S Message
  Teachers are supported by a team of learning specialists, including the librarian, the guidance counselor, and the learning support teacher, to meet the individual needs of special learners.

- ACTION ADVOCACY PLAN
  After consulting other specialists and the teacher, the librarian secures new resources to meet the needs of a new student from China who only speaks Cantonese.

Example 3

- TEACHERS care about the quality assessment of student work.

- LIBRARIAN'S Message
  The librarian will grade the selection and documentation of the sources part of the project rubric.

- ACTION ADVOCACY PLAN
  The teacher and librarian create assessment rubrics together and share grading. Student work is displayed or presented in the library.

Example 4

- TEACHERS care about learning Web 2.0 tools for more efficient teaching.

- LIBRARIAN'S Message
  The librarian can demonstrate to teachers how to use some new Web tools to improve their practice.

- ACTION ADVOCACY PLAN
  During faculty or department meetings, the librarian demonstrates a Web-based tool for teachers, providing examples of how it was used in collaboration with a classroom teacher.

While implementing the action advocacy plan with teachers, the successful school library advocate should make teachers aware of state and national legislative issues that could affect libraries. Too often, school librarians compartmentalize school library issues and do not share them with other educators. Be informative at faculty and curriculum meetings, lunch, and social gatherings. For example, some states provide libraries with state-funded subscription databases that teachers and their students use. If funding is in jeopardy, lead a discussion about the impact of this loss on students' projects and other educational needs and ask teachers to take a stand by e-mailing their legislators. When the librarian provides the contact information and a preformatted message, most teachers will act, especially if it affects the teacher's instruction and students' access to resources.

Another example of creating school library champions among teachers is the legislator visit. A librarian can schedule a visit from a legislator and invite a teacher's class(es)—perhaps a government class or an elementary class studying how a bill becomes law—to the library to talk with the legislator. Asking the teacher to reinforce with the legislator how much the school needs support for a particular school and/or library funding issue strengthens the teacher–librarian partnership. Many teachers will step forward and become library champions if the librarian informs them of what is happening and the consequences. However, if the librarian isn't informing the teachers and facilitating action, nothing is likely to happen.

Forming a school library advisory council or a Friends of the Library committee representing a few teachers, administrators, parents, students, and community/business people is another strategy for developing library champions. Surprisingly almost no school libraries have such committees according to a survey published in 2008 ("One Question" 2008, 60). This forum allows others to begin to understand the administrative side of a library program, its power in education, and the investments needed to affect student achievement. However, such a committee needs a clearly defined and focused purpose that is advisory in nature, not involved in micromanaging procedural aspects of the school library program or in making decisions normally attributed to the building principal. Some good sources to assist in creating an advisory committee or Friends of the School Library are listed under Additional Resources in this chapter.

Building Champions among Principals and District-Level Administrators

Many sources have documented that school administrators are ill prepared in the administration and fostering of quality school library programs (Lau 2002; Wilson and MacNeil 1998). The fact that most school librarians are still evaluated with a teacher evaluation form should say it all! Despite this, there are many good resources available touting how school librarians can work more effectively with principals to advocate for libraries (McGhee and Jansen 2010). Interestingly, the title of an online professional development program for school administrators offered by Mansfield University had to be changed when principals reacted to the word "advocacy." The title was "Partners for Success: School Library Advocacy for Administrators"; upon request from participating administrators, it was changed in 2008 to "Leveraging the School Libraries to Improve Student Learning" (http://libweb.mansfield.edu/promise/advocacy.asp). Principals stated they "don't do advocacy" but completely agreed with the term "leveraging."

However, principals and other administrators do advocate—or perhaps they refer to it as "promoting" or "setting priorities" for libraries—especially during closed-door budget sessions. Administrators will do their best to foster the school library program when the librarians are making a difference with students, working in tandem with teachers, and seen as an asset to the whole school. Unlike any other educator, the school librarian is often perceived to *be* the school library program. If the librarian is not seen as critical to student learning, not only is that position vulnerable to elimination but so too is the school library.

In the "Leveraging the School Libraries to Improve Student Learning" program, principals were surveyed before and after the five-week online awareness course. From 2003 to 2009, 82 principals completed the program. Prior to beginning the program, principals stated that they were not conversant or knowledgeable about five major objectives of the program:

- Describe the roles of a school librarian as identified in national guidelines (90%)
- Define information literacy (81%)
- List the inputs and guidelines needed to develop a quality school library collection (73%)
- Relate school library research to the library's impact on student learning (73%)
- Apply effective strategies in scheduling the use of the library and its program (73%) (Kachel, unpublished data 2003–2009)

Many school librarians expect their principals to know these basic tenets of a school library program; most don't. Levitov interviewed some of the principals who completed the Mansfield online program for her dissertation and determined that the short awareness program did in fact produce results. The top three major themes that emerged after taking the program were:

- Changed perceptions of the school librarian and the library program
- Improved ability to communicate with the librarian and others about the library program
- Increased awareness of what the principal could do to support the library program (Levitov 2009, 119)

The following comments expressed by principals who completed the program are typical of the comments recorded during interviews. They hint at administrator's concerns.

- "I'm stuck with how to convince my staff to let go of their predictable half hour a week to move to a flexible schedule."
- "I now see the lack of vision/purpose of our current library. I see the need to intentionally schedule for collaboration."
- "We need to help the classroom teaching staff change their philosophy of what the school librarian can be in our building. I would like to see a shift toward collaboration and toward a new thinking about the librarian's role as a teaching partner." (Kachel 2010, 47)

Working with principals, in some ways, is just like working with legislators. The school library advocate needs to "deliver the votes" on an issue before the legislator will go to the floor of the legislature and fight for a bill. Principals need school librarians to convince teachers, or at least the teacher-leaders, of a need before principals will fight at the district level for the resources to implement it. Many librarians expect principals to do all the "heavy lifting," as it is called in the legislative world, to improve the school library program. It's not going to happen; principals have far too many other

Type of Administrator	What he/she is concerned about	Relationship to the school library program	The activity/action
Principal	Test scores	Research correlates higher test scores with quality library programs	Share the research and conduct an action research project studying test scores of students who consistently use and check out library resources.
Principal	Parent involvement in the school	The library needs parent support and volunteers	In addition to offering a parent volunteer program, the librarian creates a parent resources page on the library website so parents can help their children to complete school projects.
Curriculum Coordinator	Instruction aligned with standards	Librarian wants to embed AASL 21stc learner standards with academic subject standards	The librarian volunteers to be on a curriculum committee to ensure that research and information literacy are integrated.
Technology Coordinator	Misuse of the Internet	Librarian wants students and staff to use appropriate sites and databases	Offer to co-teach a professional development program for teachers on using subscription databases.
Superintendent	Good PR in the community	Librarian needs good PR too	Librarian invites the superintendent to be the "master of ceremonies" at a Read Across America evening program she has coordinated.

Fig. 7.3.   Potential advocacy activities that target principals and other administrators.

concerns and responsibilities. Librarians need to assume the mantle of leadership and advocacy dispositions and go to work.

There are many opportunities for the school librarian to create library champions among principals and other district-level administrators (see figure 7.3). Since every school environment is different, strategies must be selected and customized to be successful. It is also important to remember that advocacy is a "planned, deliberate, sustained effort to develop understanding and support incrementally over time" (Haycock 2006). Doing one advocacy activity will not transform a school administrator into a library champion. Champions are developed over time through a consistent and persistent advocacy plan that engages the potential champion in library-related activities that are meaningful to them.

Most administrators, as well as school board members, respond positively to data and evidence. Too often school librarians say that their administrators don't ask them for any reports so they don't produce any. Administrators will not support the library program if they don't know what is happening in the library. Communication to inform, as well as to receive credit, is key. All written and e-mail communications by the librarian need a signature with title and school name. Web pages created by the librarian need to be so credited. Teacher and parent handouts, PowerPoints, and student worksheets need to minimally include the school library name and the librarian's name. Ironically, by not claiming authorship for the good work done by librarians, they perpetuate their invisibility.

A powerful tool that every school librarian should consider a job responsibility is creating an annual report and making it public to all stakeholders. The purpose is to document evidence of the success of the school library program in educating students, supporting teachers, providing instruction, and spending taxpayers' dollars effectively and wisely. The annual report should include a section on how well the librarian and program met the stated goals for the year and set new goals for the next year. The report should show trends in the collection (size, age, budget, usage, digital formats, etc.) and trends in instruction (collaboration—number of teachers and departments, classes taught, etc.). The report should highlight student projects and reading motivational programs. Charts, tables, photos, embedded short videos (on Web versions) all help to produce a visual "picture" of the year's activities. See the appendix, page 112, for "Use This Page: The Annual Report Guide" (*School Library Monthly*, May/June 2012), an extension of the article, "The Annual Report as Advocacy Tool" by Debra E. Kachel (*School Library Monthly* May/June 2012, pages 27–29).

Examples of annual reports are posted at the *School Library Websites: Examples of Effective Practice* wiki at http://schoollibrarywebsites.wikispaces.com/. Joyce Valenza, high school librarian at Springfield Township, Oreland, Pennsylvania, produces her annual report in Issuu, a free digital publishing platform (www.issuu.com) that she uploads on her library Web site (http://springfieldlibrary.wikispaces.com/). These types of public reports immediately elevate the school librarian in the eyes of others and serve as "observable" evidence of what and how a librarian contributes to the education of students.

Building Champions among School Board Members

As elected officials, school board members are chosen to represent the interests, core beliefs, and values of the local community while ensuring a high-quality education for the students in their district. Even though the position is voluntary and unpaid, board members are legally held accountable for their decisions regarding everything from balancing the budget and meeting state and federal mandates to union and personnel issues. School board members represent all the schools in the district, see the "big picture," and are concerned about equally distributing funds and services to all buildings. Therefore, if a school librarian wants something specific to his or her library, the appeal should be directed to the building principal, not the school board. To be successful advocates at a district level, district school librarians should work together to position all school library programs as essential components of every school building. This approach is ideal because there is strength in numbers and work can be shared among the librarians.

Each school board member, similar to each legislator, brings her or his own set of personal experiences and work background to the task of making policy decisions for the school district. Librarians need to do some research and get to know what board members care about, what careers they have, how influential they are in the community, where their children go to school, and so forth. Most school board meetings and public hearings are open meetings. Working together, librarians can establish a schedule for attending meetings. Librarians need to "watch and learn," initially observing how libraries might be affected by certain fiscal and state mandates. It is also important to identify various interest groups who attend and make comments at public board meetings. Listen to the concerns of community members and gauge the reaction and stance of school board members. Identify community leaders who can sway opinions of board members.

After librarians gather research about members and regular attendees of board meetings and observe how school board meetings operate, they can design a presentation aimed at the board members' interests to build influence for school library programs. Librarians should request permission to present through established district protocols, create polished presentations and/or handouts, dress and speak professionally, and be mindful of the amount of time allocated for the presentation. The focus, as always, must be on student learning, not what a librarian does and needs. If the short program is positive, upbeat, and compelling, board members will likely ask questions—perhaps opening an opportunity for librarians to state program needs. However, a public presentation directly aimed at asking the school board for more money will likely not be well received. School board members want school staff to be highly skilled and talented and make a positive impression on the community. The objective should be to showcase libraries as creative learning commons that exist to help students learn and work collaboratively on innovative projects with real-world connections. Technology and glitzy presentations work with this audience while highlighting 21st-century information and research skills. Short videos produced by or about students are always popular. Although the presentation may only be 10–15 minutes, recognize it means hours in preparation and background research. However, the investment in time is likely to pay off and highlight the leadership and advocacy skills of the librarians.

Another sure winner in capturing the attention of school administrators and board members is grant writing. School librarians need to be competent in writing grants and seeking outside sources of funding, not just in running book fairs. Again, this is a significant investment in time and research but pays huge dividends. Grant writing is a good collaborative activity whether with teachers or other librarians. These events also need to be widely publicized in local newspapers and media outlets, as well as within the school via parent and teacher newsletters. This is a win-win situation for everyone in both the school library program and the school district.

In Summary

Cultivating champions among school leaders—teachers, administrators, and school board members—takes time, patience, good people skills, and a recognition that such advocacy efforts are no longer optional if school library programs are to continue to have a presence in education and an impact on student learning. However, school librarians already possess the necessary skill sets to make this happen.

1. *Identification Skills.* School librarians are keen observers and know who the school leaders are—those whom others listen to and will follow. It is likely that the librarian is already collaborating with some of the teacher-leaders, works with the administrators who make key decisions, and can certainly

learn who among the school board members are influential. By serving on key committees and attending school board meetings, the school librarian will learn whose opinions are valued.

2. *Research Skills.* School librarians can listen to and know how to research people to discover what issues are important to stakeholders that can hook them into supporting the school library program. It may be an equity issue for board members, access to quality curricular resources for teachers, or provision of technology professional development for the teaching staff for a principal. Librarians also know how to access the findings from the school library impact studies and talking points supplied by state and national library associations, selecting ideas that will resonate with identified stakeholder groups.

3. *Communication Skills.* To nurture champions, school librarians, who admittedly are the experts on school libraries, need to provide the evidence and information about issues affecting the library program to identified champions. For example, the librarian knows the timing of the budget cycle, what state and federal bills will affect school library funding and regulations, and what resources are needed to meet the needs of learners. Librarians need to think of themselves as "campaign managers" crafting the message, preparing the "talking points," and working behind the scenes to provide the champions with the message.

Although some school librarians admit to engaging in "advocacy," sometimes the missing element is developing the understanding and support *in others*. The voices of school librarians alone are not enough to affect the type of change needed to support school library programs in today's environment. "Outside voices" from those who are not librarians need to be heard to carry the message to a broader audience. Yet these outsiders need the knowledge that librarians have about providing quality school library programs. As evidenced in Washington state, when the Washington Library Media Association (WLMA), the state's school library organization, worked with the Spokane Moms, legislative accomplishments strengthening school library programs and staffing became a reality (Whelan 2008).

While developing champions who will speak out for libraries, school librarians build their own personal and professional influence within the school and community. By embracing the advocacy and leadership dispositions identified by Bush and Jones (2011), school librarians become comfortable with these be-

Meaningful Communication

The following are resources that focus on communication with stakeholders that will provide meaningful information about the school library program:

"Use This Page: Library Advocacy through Teaching and Learning," *School Library Monthly* (January 2010): 2. See the appendix, page 109. This page provides ideas for capitalizing on opportunities to share the educational role of the school library and involve students.

"Use This Page: Tips for School Librarians—Meaningful Communication with Administrators," *School Library Monthly* (February 2010): 2. See the appendix, page 113. These tips focus on key points to consider when communicating with administrators.

haviors over time and incorporate them as habits in their practices and responsibilities as school librarians. They become the catalysts and coaches behind successful, long-term, champion-building partnerships that can result in robust and enduring school library programs for students.

References

American Association of School Librarians. *Empowering Learners: Guidelines for School Library Media Programs.* Chicago, Ill.: American Library Association, 2009.

Bush, Gail, and Jami L. Jones. "Forecasting Professional Dispositions of School Librarians." *School Library Monthly* 27, no. 4 (January 2011): 54–56.

Hartzell, Gary. *Building Influence for the School Librarian: Tenets, Targets, and Tactics.* 2nd ed. Worthington, Ohio: Linworth, 2003.

Hartzell, Gary N. "The Invisible School Librarian: Why Other Educators Are Blind to Your Value." *School Library Journal* 43, no. 11 (November 1997): 24–29.

Haycock, Ken. "Advocacy: New Views." PowerPoint, Ken Haycock & Associates, Inc. April 12, 2006. http://www.docstoc.com/docs/69774646/Advocacy-PowerPoint-Presentation (accessed December 30, 2011).

Kachel, Debra E. "Leveraging School Libraries to Support Student Learning: What Principals Need to Know." *School Library Monthly* 26, no. 9 (May 2010): 45–47.

LaRue, James. "The Visibility and Invisibility of Librarians." *Library Journal: Library News, Reviews and Views.* November 15, 2010. http://www.libraryjournal.com/lj/reviewsreference/887361-283/the_visibility_and_invisibility_of.html.csp (accessed July 26, 2011).

Lau, Debra. 2002. "What Does Your Boss Think about You?" *School Library Journal* 48, no. 9:52.

Levitov, Deborah D. *Perspectives of School Administrators Related to School Library Media Programs after Participating in an Online Course, "School Library Advocacy for Administrators."* PhD diss., University of Missouri–Columbia, 2009.

McGhee, Marla W., and Barbara A. Jansen. *The Principal's Guide to a Powerful Library Media Program.* 2nd ed. Worthington, Ohio: Linworth, 2010.

"One Question Survey Results [Do You Have a Library Advisory Committee?]." *Library Media Connection* 26, no. 6 (March 2008): 60.

"Portrait of the Guardian." *Kiersey.com.* http://www.keirsey.com/4temps/guardian_overview.asp (accessed September 23, 2011).

"Use This Page: The Annual Report Guide." *School Library Monthly* 28, no. 8 (May/June 2012): 2.

"Use This Page: Library Advocacy through Teaching and Learning." *School Library Monthly* 27, no. 4 (January 2010): 2.

"Use This Page: Tips for School Librarians—Meaningful Communication with Administrators." *School Library Monthly* 27, no. 5 (February 2010): 2.

"Use This Page: Tips on Using *The School Library Link* in Your School." *School Library Monthly* 26, no. 3 (November 2009): 2

Whelan, Debra Lau. "Three Spokane Moms Save Their School Libraries." *School Library Journal* (September 1, 2008).

Wilson, Patricia Potter, and Angus J. MacNeil. "In the Dark: What's Keeping Principals from Understanding Libraries?" *School Library Journal* 44, no. 9 (September 1998): 114–16.

Additional Resources

Bush, Gail, and Jami Biles Jones. *Tales Out of the School Library: Developing Professional Dispositions.* Santa Barbara, Calif.: Libraries Unlimited, 2010.

DelGuidice, Margaux. "When a Leadership Opportunity Knocks, Answer!" *Library Media Connection* (October 2011): 47–49.

DelGuidice, Margaux, and Rose Luna. *Make a Big Impact @ Your School Board Meeting*. Santa Barbara, Calif.: Libraries Unlimited, 2012.

"Fund Our Future Washington." http://www.fundourfuturewashington.org/ (accessed September 30, 2011).

Hartzell, Gary. "How Do Decision Makers Become Library Media Advocates?" *Knowledge Quest* 36, no. 1 (September 2007): 32–35.

Harvey, Carl. "Environment Matters." *School Library Monthly* 26, no. 7 (March 2010): 15–16.

Harvey, Carl. "The New Boss!" *School Library Monthly* 28, no. 5 (February 2012): 13–15.

Harvey, Carl. "Under the Radar." *School Library Media Activities Monthly* 24, no. 10 (June 2008): 47-48.

Kachel, Debra E. "The Annual Report as an Advocacy Tool." *School Library Monthly* 28, no. 8 (May/June 2012): 27–29.

Levitov, Deborah D. "Educating School Administrators." *School Library Monthly* 26, no. 6 (February 2010): 45–47.

Moreillon, Judi, and Kristin Fontichiaro. "Getting off the Ground Floor: Back-to-School Elevator Speeches." *Knowledge Quest* 38, no. 1 (September 2009): 74–76.

Public Education Network and American Association of School Librarians. *The Information-Powered School*. Ed. Sandra Hughes-Hassel and Anne Wheelock, 105–13. Chicago: American Library Association, 2001. Chapter 10: Community Engagement for Information Power. "Library Advisory Committee." Chart entitled "Building Your Library Advisory Committee" located at http://www.publiceducation.org/pdf/HS_Libraries/Building_Your_Library_Advisory_Committee.doc (accessed December 31, 2011).

"Sample Job Description Title: School Librarian." American Association of School Librarians, 2010. http://www.ala.org/ala/mgrps/divs/aasl/guidelinesandstandards/learning4life/resources/sample_job_description_L4L.pdf (accessed September 30, 2011).

South Carolina State Department of Education. "Library Media Center Advisory Committees." http://ed.sc.gov/agency/pr/Standards-and-Curriculum/old/Instructional-Promising-Practices/Library-Media-Services/LMCManagement.html (accessed September 23, 2011).

Teske, Natalie. "Library Advisory Councils." *Library Media Connection* 28, no. 4 (January 2010): 40–41.

Designing Learning for Evidence-Based Practice

This chart accompanies the article "Designing Learning for Evidence-Based Practice" by Marjorie L. Pappas (*SLMAM*, January 2008: 19-23).

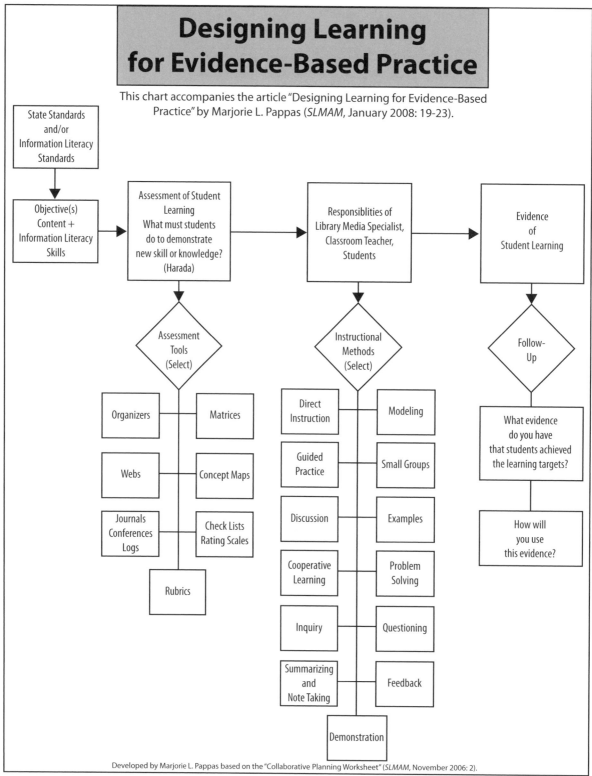

State Standards and/or Information Literacy Standards

Objective(s) Content + Information Literacy Skills

Assessment of Student Learning
What must students do to demonstrate new skill or knowledge? (Harada)

Responsiblities of Library Media Specialist, Classroom Teacher, Students

Evidence of Student Learning

Assessment Tools (Select)

Organizers
Matrices
Webs
Concept Maps
Journals Conferences Logs
Check Lists Rating Scales
Rubrics

Instructional Methods (Select)

Direct Instruction
Modeling
Guided Practice
Small Groups
Discussion
Examples
Cooperative Learning
Problem Solving
Inquiry
Questioning
Summarizing and Note Taking
Feedback
Demonstration

Follow-Up

What evidence do you have that students achieved the learning targets?

How will you use this evidence?

Developed by Marjorie L. Pappas based on the "Collaborative Planning Worksheet" (*SLMAM*, November 2006: 2).

Inquiry-based Teaching and Learning— The Role of the Library Media Specialist

by Barbara Stripling

An extension of "Inquiry: Inquiring Minds Want to Know" (*SLMAM*, September 2008: 50-52).

Collaboration

Collaboration underpins the success of any library media program. The library media specialist and classroom teachers must support each other because inquiry takes more time, the path may be unpredictable, the teacher is not always in control, students need a lot of support throughout the process, students need resources beyond the classroom on an unpredictable variety of subjects, and amid all the complexities, students must be surrounded by a safe and well-organized learning environment.

Through collaboration, the library media specialist can:

- ►Help restructure the curriculum so that inquiry and problem solving are integrated into all subject areas.
- ►Foster connections across curriculum areas, a focus on broad concepts instead of isolated facts, and the true blending of content and process.
- ►Incorporate the American Association for School Librarians (AASL) *Standards for the 21st-Century Learner*.

Teaching

The goal of inquiry-based teaching is that all students develop an "inquiry stance" with more emphasis on asking good questions than finding the answers (Cochran-Smith and Lytle 1999).

Library media specialists can:

- ►Establish a learner-centered environment by gradually releasing responsibility to the students.
- ►Integrate the teaching of habits of mind (Audet and Jordan 2005, 89-90) with inquiry and communication skills to foster both active and reflective learning.
- ►Enhance students' effectiveness in learning when they pay attention to the learning environment of the library and attend to four main areas that comprise a climate that fosters inquiry (Bransford, Brown, and Cocking 1999, 121):

  1. Learners' skills, attitudes, prior knowledge, interests.
  2. Knowledge formation through connections among ideas, focus on big concepts and intriguing questions, integration of skills and dispositions.
  3. Assessment by both teacher and student of process and content of learning.
  4. Community of learners that surround the learning experiences with sharing, interchange of ideas, listening to and challenging the ideas of others.

- ►Scaffold and support students through the difficult process of inquiry, but also challenge superficial ideas and uncritical acceptance of evidence if students are to reach as high as they can in their learning (Donham 2001, 3).
- ►Integrate and implement AASL's *Standards for the 21st-Century Learner*.

Collection Development

Inquiry is obviously dependent on availability of instructional materials and equipment. Inquiry is, in fact, a major incentive for a school to invest in a library media center.

Library media specialists can:

- ►Provide both physical and virtual resources that are tied closely to curriculum areas of emphasis by involving teachers in the selection process. For example, Web sites that are particularly good for specific units can be made available for easy access through the library home page, wikis, portals, and special bookmarking sites like *del.icio.us*.
- ►Place special emphasis on providing access to multiple perspectives and on offering materials for in-depth study, not superficial grazing.
- ►Advocate for technology that is essential for access to a wide variety of resources.
- ►Assist in providing guidance and instruction in the use of technology for learning.
- ►Assist in providing guidance in the use of books and periodicals.
- ►Assist in incorporating students' use of technology for inquiry learning involving social tools to share and build on the ideas of others, and to demonstrate their learning to a broader community.

Leadership and Professional Development

In effective professional development, teachers are guided to (National Research Council 2000, 91-98):

- ►Do inquiry themselves multiple times;
- ►Reflect on their own inquiry experiences;
- ►Develop conceptual understanding of their content area and of inquiry;
- ►Be a part of a collaborative community of inquiry;
- ►Assess their own teaching practices and content priorities in terms of effectiveness of student learning; and
- ►Rethink instructional time to build in inquiry experiences.

Library media specialists can:

- ►Provide professional development (in the form of workshops, study groups, mentoring, or collaborative planning) that offers teachers opportunities to participate in inquiry-based experiences and hone their own skills and confidence in inquiry-based teaching.
- ►Take a leadership role in fostering inquiry throughout their school community by communicating with administrators about the attributes and requirements of inquiry-based teaching and learning, so that the administrators support teachers and foster a schoolwide culture of inquiry.
- ►Seize every opportunity to reach out to parents and interpret inquiry-based teaching and learning for them through newsletters, parent/teacher conference nights, special workshops and programs, and presentations of student projects (Inquiry Nights).

See reference list on page 52 in this issue of *SLMAM*.◄

Join Kristin Fontichiaro at the *SLMAM* blog for ongoing discussion and information related to AASL's *Standards for 21st-Century Learner* (http://blog.schoollibrarymedia.com/).

Use This Page

Taking Action: Saving School Libraries

This chart is intended to help school librarians work with others to address the six steps outlined by Allison Zmuda in her article "Six Steps to Saving Your School Library Program" (pages 45-48). Each step will require a unique approach for every program. The questions and suggestions found in this chart will require revision for each setting. Resources should be identified that will assist in each step (e.g., current literature, expertise, research).

Six Steps: Saving Your School Library Program

1. To Do:	Review	Revise	Implement Changes	Evaluate
Mission Statement	What is the purpose? Is student learning the central focus?	What are the key words? What will students be able to do? Who will be involved?	Finalize. Share. Put it into action.	How is the mission statement used? How does it support student learning? What difference does it make?
2. To Do:	**Review**	**Revise**	**Implement Changes**	**Evaluate**
Program Alignment	What are the policies? What are the practices? What is the structure? How is student learning supported? Which policies are embraced/resisted by stakeholders?	How can learning be better supported? What is a learning commons? How can space be used differently/better? What kind of access and tools are needed?	Identify needs (e.g., time, money, revision, re-envisioning, professional development, resources, etc.) and act. Follow a timeline.	How do new policies and practices support student learning? How is space used differently and better? What changes have resulted in addressing access and use of tools?
3. To Do:	**Review**	**Revise**	**Implement Changes**	**Evaluate**
Student Learning	What student assessments are used? What is the nature of student learning via the library? What input do you receive?	How can assessments be improved to examine student learning? How is learning meaningful? What will be done to gather input?	Identify inquisitive and dynamic learning. Determine assessments. Arrange for professional evaluation and feedback.	What are the differences in student learning? How are assessments appropriate? How has input and feedback been used?
4. To Do:	**Review**	**Revise**	**Implement Changes**	**Evaluate**
Quality Tasks in the School Library	How are tasks supportive of student learning? How do tasks support the mission statement? How do tasks align with curriculum and national visioning documents?	How can learning be improved? What assessments can be used? What is the instructional intent? What are quality tasks?	Work with teachers to improve student learning. Use defined learning tasks as a guide. Use appropriate assessments.	Is student work authentic? How are definitions being met? How are tasks meaningful? What needs improvement?
5. To Do:	**Review**	**Revise**	**Implement Changes**	**Evaluate**
Instructional Time	What is the online presence? How does the library extend services beyond the school day?	What tools are available? What have others done? What resources will help? What online learning options are possible?	Identify possibilities. Know the purpose. Identify learning benefits. Follow a timeline.	What is the impact for students? What do colleagues think? What works? What can be improved?
6. To Do:	**Review**	**Revise**	**Implement Changes**	**Evaluate**
Know the Brain	What do you know about cognition and learning? How can you learn more? What resources will help?	How can students be more engaged? How can learning be more meaningful? How can students be helped to focus?	Identify expectations. Identify strategies. Work with others. Involve students. Get feedback.	In what ways are students more engaged? How is learning more meaningful? In what ways are students more focused?

Assessment Tool: Levels of Communication, Cooperation, and Collaboration with Teachers

Use this chart to record the work you do with teachers over the course of the year. It will give you data to identify successes and gains as well as possible gaps. It will help you think about new approaches and set goals for the future. Compiled and summarized, it can provide important information to share with administrators about your work.

Identify the level of the working relationship with the teacher for:	Cooperation	Coordination	Collaboration
Instructional Design			
Execution of Instruction			
Assessment of Student Work			
Reflection and Improvement			

Relationship
What do you want to remember?

Comments:

Teacher's Name:	Grade Level:	Date:	Curriculum Area:

Developed by Deborah Levitov in collaboration with Allison Zmuda (See Zmuda's article "Where Does Your Authority Come From?: Empowering the Library Media Specialist as a True Partner in Student Achievement," *SLMAM*, September 2006: 19-22). For more understanding of this page, see the articles: "When Does Collaboration Start?" by Gail Dickeson (*SLMAM*, October 2006: 56-57); and "Collaboration Practices" by Carolyn S. Brodie (*SLMAM*, October 2006: 27-30).

Assessing the Research Process

Lesson plans usually list identified learning goals and these often include inquiry and information literacy objectives. Assessment tools may be developed, but they do not always address the inquiry and information literacy skills specifically. This rubric is meant to be a starting point for school librarians when developing assessments for the research process. It is an overview of what should be taken into consideration. The actual wording and the listed learning objectives would reflect specific lesson plans (see another rubric example on page 8).

Rubric for Assessing the Research Objectives				
Learning Objectives:	**Beginning Ability**	**Developing Proficiency**	**Skilled Proficiency**	**Outstanding Proficiency**
Identifying the Topic	Unable to choose a topic.	A topic is chosen with significant help.	A topic is chosen with little help.	A topic is chosen independently.
Developing Questions	Unable to develop questions.	Yes-no questions identified—help needed to expand.	Open-ended questions are developed with little help.	Open-ended questions are developed independently.
Finding Resources	Unable to identify and locate resources.	Identifies and locates resources with significant help.	Locates appropriate resources with minimal help.	Locates appropriate resources independently.
Addressing Questions	Unable to identify and record relevant information.	Identifies and records relevant information with significant help.	Identifies and records relevant information with minimal help.	Identifies and records relevant information independently.
Evaluating Resources	Unable to identify information as reliable, accurate, and current.	Identifies information as reliable, accurate and current with significant help.	Identifies information as reliable, accurate and current with minimal help.	Independently identifies information as reliable, accurate and current.
Citing Sources	No sources are cited.	Only one source is cited with assistance.	More than one source is cited independently but there are errors in citation.	Multiple sources are cited without error.
Time on Task	Many reminders are required and work is not completed.	Many time reminders are required but work is completed.	Minimal time reminders necessary but work is completed on time.	Time is wisely used and work is completed on time.

School Library Monthly/Volume XXVI, Number 4/December 2009

Planning and Assessing Inquiry-based Learning

When planning instruction with classroom teachers, school librarians can use the following questions to guide instructional design and evaluate success in meeting learning objectives through an inquiry process. Discussing these questions with collaborative partners can either affirm inquiry-level teaching and learning or nudge instructional design toward it. For more information, see the articles "Nudging toward Inquiry: Re-envisioning Existing Research Projects" (pages 17-19) and "Nudging toward Inquiry: Re-envisioning the Biography Report" (page 5) in this issue of *SLM*.

▶ What should students learn?

What are the learning objectives?
What are the needed skills?
Is this lesson focused on skill-building, or is it a performance task in which students demonstrate what they have learned?
How will the educators guide the inquiry process?
How will learning strategies be provided or reinforced?

▶ How will students learn?

How will students be independent and self-reliant, and make choices?
How will students be actively engaged in questioning, problem-solving, and learning?
How will students create and answer essential questions?
How will students apply new information?
How will students articulate what they have learned?
Will students learn collaboratively or independently?
Will there be opportunities for peer feedback?
How will students reflect on the process and learning?
How will students understand how to improve?
What will students take away from this experience and transfer to new situations?

▶ How will educators know if students learned the information?

How will students demonstrate proficiency (skills)?
How will students demonstrate understanding (performance)?
How will evidence of learning be provided?
How will students self-assess?
How will the educators assess product and process?

▶ Other "Use This Page" articles that compliment this effort:

"Steps to Designing Inquiry-based Units" (*SLMAM*, November 2008, page 2)
"Assessing Questions" (*SLMAM*, January 2009, page 2)
"Collaborative Planning" (*SLMAM*, November 2006, page 2)

Data-Driven Program Development: A Quick Guide

THIS GUIDE IS derived from Ann Martin's article, "Data-Driven Leadership" (pages 31-33) in this issue of *SLM*. It serves as a quick reference tool for school librarians when processing Martin's article and putting concepts to work for data-driven program improvement and support.

EXAMPLES FOR DATA GATHERING:

►SURVEYS:
One-on-one conversations
Group discussions
Online surveys
Follow-up surveys

►COLLECTION ANALYSIS:
Targeted Usage Statistics—Share specific usage statistics with administrators to support initiative and validate that money is well spent. It can also provide foundational information to request more funding for specific segments of a collection.

►CAUSE AND EFFECT ANALYSIS:
A fishbone diagram (http://quality.enr.state.nc.us/tools/fishbone.htm) is a tool that analyzes cause and effect. In the head of fish, list the issue being examined (e.g., using GPS devices for instruction), then identify areas that will impact implementation (e.g., procedures, people, policies, and skills) and place these in the bones of the fish. Add concerns by each impact word (Martin, page 32).

Next, brainstorm solutions and present them as they relate to each of the concerns listed in the bones of the dia-

gram. As a result, the data derived from the cause-and-effect analysis can serve to be convincing evidence for the proposed goal (see Figure 1, page 33).

HOW TO USE DATA:

►Use data to confirm needs (e.g., adding current authors into the library collection or materials for pre-K students). Then confirm the importance of money spent through statistics (e.g., circulation statistics) and an end-of-the-year survey.

►Use data to show how funding for the library will benefit other departments/teams in the school.

DATA ORGANIZATIONAL TIPS:

►DATA LEAD TO:
Rationale for proposed changes or programs
New ideas
Support for initiatives (initial and ongoing)
Insight into the educational connections and potential for school library/librarian

►PRESENTATION:
Use one page for the proposal summary and include: school library vision, mission, key connections to school improvement, positive impact on students and staff.
Provide a timeline for implementation.
Include a separate page with collected data to support the one-page summary and timeline
Choose wisely to whom you will present—think it through.

►FOLLOW-UP:
Have a plan for follow-up, collecting data through the program process.
Provide a summary report using statistics to verify and show impact after underway.

Advocacy 101

As the articles in this issue of SLM convey, advocacy is not a choice, it is a necessity. The following is a list of reminders as well as resources that can help school librarians focus on activism and provide helpful resources. Tack this up where you will see it daily; set goals; act; evaluate progress; make it continuous.

REMEMBER:

► Advocacy is necessary and must be ongoing. See the AASL Toolkits: http://www.ala.org/ala/mgrps/divs/aasl/aaslissues/toolkits/toolkits.cfm.

► It is never too late to educate—don't assume that administrators, teachers, or others know and understand school libraries of today.

► Be proactive—have an elevator speech and a long-term plan.

► Use research and data—gather and share it often.

► Show connections that impact education and learning—how the library education program addresses school improvement and academic plans.

► Build a program with evidence-based practice—figure out how to show what students are learning because of the school library program and the school librarian.

► Don't underestimate leadership—it is a requirement for school librarians.

RESOURCES:

► "Furloughed but Not Forgotten" by Debra E. Kachel, *SLM*/Februrary 2012, pages 5-7.

► Articles posted under "Advocate/Advocacy" on the *SLM* website: http://schoollibrarymonthly.com/articles/index.html
These articles offer many sound ideas from leaders in the field that will help accomplish advocacy. Additional articles are available in print versions of *SLM/SLMAM* since September 2005.

► ACT 4 School Libraries: http://schoollibrarymonthly.com/act4sl.html
This tri-fold provides talking points and the site has many helpful links.

► *The Many Faces of School Library Leadership*, Sharon Coatney, Editor. (Libraries Unlimited, 2010).
The chapters in this book will help build leadership skills and provide ideas to plan for and build leadership potential.

► *SLM* "Use This Page" with an Advocacy focus:
  ▷ Advocacy Planning: Vision, Voice, Visibility, and Vigilance (PDF)
  ▷ *SLM*/January 2012
  ▷ Data-Driven Program Development: A Quick Guide (PDF)
  ▷ *SLM*/November 2011
  ▷ *SLM*: 09/2009; 12/2009; 01/2010; 02/2010
  ▷ *SLMAM*: 02/2007; 10/2006; 11/2007; 01/2008

Advocacy Planning:
Vision, Voice, Visibility, and Vigilance

In the two-part article (*SLM* December, 2011 and January 2012), "Creating a Districtwide Advocacy Plan, Parts 1 & 2," Christie Kaaland presents four key components necessary for creating district advocacy plans for school libraries: Vision, Voice, Visibility, and Vigilance. Below is a summary of the four components.

DISTRICTWIDE ADVOCACY PLANNING

I. THE VISION FOR SCHOOL LIBRARIES
Create a shared mission (involve others) and incorporate:
- Student Achievement
- District Focus
- Unique Attributes of the District
- Local Strengths
- Strategic Connections to Local Interests
- Memorable Language
- Fresh Perspectives

II. THE VOICE OF THE ADVOCATE
What: Identify Library and Curriculum Connections
Where and When: Create a Strategic Plan for Presentations
How: Be Positive, Energetic, Constructive, Convincing, Ambitious
Who: Carefully Choose Spokespersons (e.g., students, teachers, community members, etc.)

III. VISIBILITY
Physical Visibility
- Create a High Profile (make it meaningful—what does it say about the library program?)
- Be Involved in Curriculum Planning
- Attend and Present at Parent Meetings
- Be a Presence at School Events (e.g., curriculum nights, school events, plays, etc.)
- Have a Presence at School Board Meetings

Virtual Visibility
- Use Technology to Showcase the Library Program
- Carefully Plan the Web Image (friendly faces, inviting spaces, learning-centered)
- Keep It Current
- Make It Manageable
- Take Advantage of 24/7

IV. VIGILANCE

Work For:
- Sustained Success (pervasive and long lasting)
- Substance (meaningful and perpetual)
- Ongoing Effort (evaluate, revise, redo)

Library Advocacy through Teaching and Learning

Use this page as an extension of the lesson plan "Saving at Your School Library" by Christie Kaaland on pages 7-9. Kaaland developed the list to demonstrate how this assignment can be used as an advocacy tool. Never miss an opportunity to let your school, community, and families know about the opportunities the school library provides.

Advocacy efforts may include:

 Announce cost-saving results throughout the school:
  ▷Display on all-school reader boards.
  ▷Include a paragraph in parent newsletters ("Did you know…").
  ▷Post on school and/or library Web site.
Be sure to mention this was done as a library math assignment.

 Share results with those that influence policy and fiscal decision-makers: Have students write individual letters to their legislators sharing their library-use cost saving.

 Additionally, superintendents love getting letters from students. This is particularly effective in districts where library personnel and/or library material cuts are being made.

 If you know there is a central administrator who is a strong library advocate in your district—whether it's the technology director or assistant superintendent of curriculum—share your results to give that advocate another reason (and ammunition) to continue support.

 Final teacher and school librarian collaboration: The teacher and school librarian together should present the assignment results to the school board or at the very least to the school's Parent-Teacher executive board.

Creating a Parent Advocacy Plan

This page is meant to help library media specialists create a parent advocacy plan. The ultimate goal is to recruit parents as advocates for the library media program. This can be accomplished, over time, through education and exposure to the benefits offered by the library media center for them and their children.

Ask Yourself:

What are the concerns of the parents in your school community?

How can the library media center meet those needs/concerns?

What are the library media services/programs/instructional efforts that benefit parents and their children?

How can you communicate with parents about the benefits of the library media program?

If you were to ask parents about the library media program, what would they say?

Getting Started:

Make a List of Parent Concerns:	Make a List of Library Media Center Concerns:
For Example:	**For Example:**
Success for their child in school and in the future	Library media center connections to curriculum and learning
Help and resources for homework	Integrated information literacy skills
Knowing what is available	Budget and staffing for the library media center
Ease of access to resources and information	Parent support
Other:	Other:

What benefits can be provided by the library media center for parents? (Match these to their concerns):

- Library media center connections to school improvement planning
- Information literacy skills and strategies
- Ease of access and organization— simple and remote
- Resource and learning links to curriculum objectives
- Parenting resources & information

Other:

What services/programs can be provided by the library media center for parents? (Match these to their concerns):

- Communication—newsletters, notes home, website postings
- Resource availability—remote online catalog, databases, website links, community links
- Tools and strategies for accomplishing homework assignments—website postings
- Parenting materials/resources for checkout—parent library, general collection, weblinks
- Presentations and programs--open house, literacy night, parent meetings, volunteer opportunities, etc.

Other:

Resources Available for Parent Advocacy:

INFOhio: http://www.infohio.org (To access the Parent's Page on the INFOhio website, click on "PARENT" on the menu at the top of the page. Be sure to take a look at the INFOhio Parent Tool Kit by going to: http://www.infohio.org/Parent/Toolkit.html.)

American Association of School Librarians (AASL) Advocacy page: http://www.ala.org/aaslTemplate.cfm?Section=aasladvocacy (Access the AASL advocacy page for ideas and information about advocacy.)

School Library Media Activities Monthly articles related to parent advocacy:

"Enlist the Choir" by Catherine M. Beyers (*SLMAM*, October 2005: 47-48).

"Looking from All Perspectives!" by Carl A. Harvey II (*SLMAM*, November 2005: 44-46).

"Families and Family Life" by Carolyn S. Brodie and Greg Byerly (*SLMAM*, December, 2005: 38-40).

"Parent Partnership Power" by Catherine M. Beyers (*SLMAM*, February 2006: 47-48).

"Plugged In @ your library®" by Catherine M. Beyers (*SLMAM*, May 2006: 49-50).

"Internet Safety Night Brought to You by the Library Media Specialist" by Maureen Tannetta (*SLMAM*, October 2006: 31-32).

"Collective Action @ your library®" by Catherine M. Beyers (*SLMAM*, January 2007: 48-50).

"Connecting the Library Media Center" and Parents by Carl A. Harvey II (*SLMAM*, February 2007:25-27).

"The INFOhio Parent Project: Models to Use" by Carolyn S. Brodie (*SLMAM*, February 2007:49-50).

Help Your Kids Evaluate Web Sites

From *The School Library Link*: http://www.theschoollibrarylink.com/

Do you help your kids do research online? Here are some tips to help guide your children to Web sites that are factual and trustworthy.

1 When you look at a Web site, look past the design and domain name. Your first stop should be the author of the Web site. Who wrote this information? What are his or her credentials?

2 Double-check your facts. Never use only one Web site to do research! Always use several sources of information to verify facts.

3 Use different search engines, rather than just Google. Try these search engines, which have been designed using reliable, kid-friendly Web site results: http://www.kidsclick.org, http://www.yahooligans.com, and http://www.askkids.com.

4 Help your kids remember to write down the Web site where they found their information. Don't know how to cite it? Try using http://www.bibme.com or come to the school library for a quick lesson on writing Webliographies.

Tips on Using *The School Library Link* in Your School

http://www.theschoollibrarylink.com/

1. Simply download it, print it out, and send it home with students once a month. Easy!

2. To save money, duplicate the newsletter in black and white. Print it on colorful paper instead.

3. "Link" the newsletter to your library by attaching a sticker with your library's contact information in the space provided.

4. Attach a second page, or a postcard, to send home information about your upcoming events or new books in the library.

5. No money for copying? Link the latest issue to your online catalog, or to your school's Web site.

6. Add a submission to your school's print newsletter: "Help your kids get the most out of the information explosion! Visit http://www.theschoollibrarylink.com."

7. Budget barebones to the max? Print out one copy of the newsletter each month and post it in your library.

The boomark (left) is created from Michelle McGarry's newsletter for parents, *The School Library Link* (see her article in this issue of *SLM*, pages 45-47). McGarry encourages school librarians to share her newsletter with parents.

The Annual Report Guide

by DEBRA E. KACHEL

The following chart, created by Debra E. Kachel, summarizes information addressed in her article "The Annual Report as an Advocacy Tool" on pages 27-29. School librarians can use the chart and article to guide the development of an annual report to be shared with others. It is an important advocacy tool that helps succinctly communicate what is being accomplished through the school library.

THE ANNUAL REPORT – Examples of Included Topics		
Objective (what you want to show)	**Data or Collection Tools** (what data you analyze)	**Examples of Evidence/Outcomes** (what goes in the report)
TEACHING FOR LEARNING		
Instruction of 21st-century skills that students need and use in all curricular areas and for lifetime learning	• Results of standardized tests (particularly reading and writing) • Info Literacy Curriculum aligned to state and national standards • Assessment tool showing mastery level of targeted skills by grade level	• TEXT—Highlight one unit, listing info literacy skills and content standards assessed; improvements on reading test scores from previous years due to targeted, collaborative instruction • PERSONAL—Quotes from students about the skills they learned and used elsewhere • WEBSITE LINKS—Info lit curriculum and/or assessment tool (macro data only, no individual names of students or teachers)
Instructional partnering with teachers to improve learning experiences for students	• Recorded schedule of collaborative instruction and library activities (schedule book or online tool)	• VISUAL—Chart showing # of integrated lessons/units taught by subject and grade level • PERSONAL—Photo or video of students presenting and/or their completed projects
BUILDING THE LEARNING ENVIRONMENT		
Instruction and support for teachers that improves instruction and student learning	• Professional development completed by librarian • Staff development time spent teaching teachers • Technology • Resources	• TEXT—List of topics taught in afterschool sessions to teachers; webinars completed by the librarian • PERSONAL—Photo of teachers learning a new computer program with librarian instructing • WEBSITE LINKS—Teacher and librarian produced web quests, wikis, etc.
Resources that improve students' reading abilities and instill a habit of reading for pleasure and to learn	• Collection and circulation data • Special reading promotions and activities	• TEXT—Short description of new units designed to address specific skills for which students tested poorly (i.e., identifying the main point, summarizing, etc.) • VISUAL—Photo of author visit or reading contest • WEBSITE LINKS—Posted "Best Reads" lists and student blog
Economical use of funds to meet school and student needs	• Budget and purchased resources • Needs assessment data (from students, teachers, curriculum mapping, etc.)	• TEXT—Summary of a student reading interest survey; trends in use of print vs. digital resources • VISUAL—Chart or bar graph of use of resources and technologies, etc.
EMPOWERING LEARNING THROUGH LEADERSHIP		
Leadership in implementing school and library mission	• Committee work of the librarian • Articles written • Grants and fundraising activities	• TEXT—List of committees and activities • WEBSITE LINKS—Links to articles placed in school newsletter or local paper by the librarian
Achieving objectives; setting new objectives	• Library use and circulation data • Student/teacher/parent surveys or focus groups	• TEXT—Assessment of needs and program trends; assessment of how well objectives have been met; state objectives for next year

Tips for School Librarians—Meaningful Communication with Administrators

For more information about communicating with administrators and taking a leadership role, see the articles "Leadership Is about You" (pages 42-44) and "Educating School Administrators" (pages 45-47) in this issue of *SLM*.

►Do Your Homework

▷Know what is important to administrator—their priorities, top concerns, plans.

▷Use their language and match their interests, needs, and priorities—avoid library jargon (e.g., L4L, information literacy, collection development, weeding, etc.).

▷Understand how the school library can support school improvement plans, staff development needs, and student needs.

▷Keep up-to-date on current trends, technologies, and district/building initiatives, and identify school library connections.

►Communicate

▷Schedule ongoing meetings, but use the time wisely, make it worthwhile, be positive, and have solutions.

▷Send an email, drop a note, or provide a newsletter.

▷Involve them in decision-making, but provide a plan and make connections to student learning goals and teachers' needs.

▷Build communication around goals for program improvement and evaluation and professional evaluation—make it forward thinking.

►Show Them

▷Provide examples of evidence-based practice—show student learning through the school library.

▷Show results and successes related to goals and objectives (e.g., program, student learning, professional development).

▷Give credit where credit is due—with examples of collaboration, teamwork, and involvement of others.

▷Show connections between collection development and curriculum objectives.

▷Provide examples of student and teacher feedback (e.g., exit slips, surveys, notes).

Index

Note: Information in figures is indicated by *f*.

About the Editor and Contributors

Sarah Applegate is a National Board Certified teacher-librarian at River Ridge High School in Lacey, Washington, where she has taught since 1995. Sarah is active in the Washington Library Media Association and has been regional chair, senior-level chair, co-advocacy chair, and president. Sarah is an adjunct faculty member for the Antioch University–Seattle Library Media Endorsement Program. She is the lead facilitator for her district's National Board Certification Cohort. Sarah recently completed a Fulbright Research grant in Finland, where she studied how Finnish schools teach information literacy skills. Sarah is an active reviewer for *Library Media Connection*.

Gail Bush, PhD, is a professor in the College of Education, director of the school library program, and director of the Center for Teaching through Children's Books at National Louis University, Chicago, Illinois. Gail's academic background includes a bachelor's degree in anthropology, master's degree in library science, and doctorate in educational psychology. Gail represents the United States as a delegate to the School Libraries and Resource Centers Standing Committee of the International Federation of Library Associations and served as the 2010–2011 president of the Illinois Library Association. A frequent speaker, Gail also publishes in both education and library journals. Recent publications include *Knowledge Quest* 38, no. 1: "The Issue is Questions" (AASL, September, 2009; guest editor); *Best of KQ: Civic Engagement, Social Justice and Equity* (AASL, 2009; edited volume); and *Tales Out of the School Library: Dispositions in Action* (ABC-CLIO, 2010; coauthored with Dr. Jami Jones).

Margaux DelGuidice, MLS, is a school librarian at Garden City High School in New York. She also works part-time as a Children's Services librarian at the Freeport Memorial Library in her hometown of Freeport, New York, and is an adjunct professor of academic writing and research at St. Joseph's College. A former ALA/EBSCO Conference Scholarship recipient, she was also one of five librarians in the country selected to be a GALE/Cengage New Leader and has served ALA as a member of the Future Perfect Task Force. She has been published *in Library Media Connection*, *School Library Monthly*, and *Knowledge Quest*. With her colleague Rose Luna, she is the coauthor of the book, *Make a Big Impact @ Your School Board Meeting* (Libraries Unlimited, 2012). Currently, she is speaking with Rose Luna at state and national library conferences on the importance of advocating for library programs by presenting at school board meetings.

Christie Kaaland (BA, Pacific Lutheran University; MA Ed, EdD, University of Washington) has taught every grade, K–adult. She spent 17 years teaching junior and senior high English and drama in the Tacoma School District before finding her true calling as an elementary librarian. It was there Kaaland first became interested in developing a school library program at Antioch University, Seattle, where she has been full-time faculty for 11 years. In her current advocacy work, Kaaland is a founding member of a national grassroots effort, Act4SL, in cooperation with school library advocate leaders from around the country working toward school libraries' inclusion in national legislative educational reform. She has written numerous articles on school library advocacy.

Debra E. Kachel served as a school librarian and library department supervisor for over 30 years and currently is an online instructor in the School Library and Information Technologies Graduate School, Mansfield University (Pennsylvania). She serves as the co-chairperson of the Legislation Committee for the Pennsylvania School Librarians Association and is a member of the Legislation Committee of the American Association of School Librarian (AASL), chairing the committee responsible for the content of the AASL Advocacy brochures. As an avid grant writer, Debra has written and administered several federal scholarship grants and currently is directing a research grant in Pennsylvania with the Keith Curry Lance and fellow researchers to determine the costs and benefits of school library infrastructures that most contribute to higher levels of student learning.

Deborah D. Levitov, PhD, is managing editor of *School Library Monthly*. She was a school librarian and coordinator of Library Media Services for Lincoln Public Schools for a total of 27 years. Her dissertation (2009) was *Perspectives of School Administrators Related to School Library Media Programs after Participating in an Online Course, "School Library Advocacy for Administrators."* She is a past president of the Nebraska Educational Media Association. She worked on the ALA @ your library campaign related to school libraries, leading a 3M-AASL 2003 training workshop for the School @ Your Library campaign. She served as chair of the AASL @ Your Library Special Committee and the AASL Advocacy Committee and served as an AASL Advocacy Institute presenter. In addition to authoring articles on advocacy, she contributed the chapter "The School Librarian as an Advocacy Leader" in *The Many Faces of School Library Leadership*, edited by Sharon Coatney (Libraries Unlimited, 2010).

Rose Luna, MLS, MSA, has been a school librarian at Freeport High School in Freeport, New York, for over 13 years. She works part-time as a bilingual reference librarian at Freeport Memorial Library in Freeport, New York, where she also leads a Spanish-language book club. Rose has published in *Knowledge Quest* and is coauthor, with Margaux DelGuidice, of the book, *Make a Big Impact @ Your School Board Meeting* (Libraries Unlimited, 2012), and she serves on the ALA Publications Committee. Currently, she is speaking with Margaux DelGuidice at state and national library conferences on the importance of advocating for library programs by presenting at school board meetings.

Ann M. Martin, MA in education and human development from George Washington University, is currently the educational specialist for library services for Henrico County Public Schools in Henrico, Virginia. She is a past president of the American Association of School Librarians (AASL) and a Virginia Educational Media Association past president. She currently is chair of the Knowledge Quest Editorial Board for the American Association of School Librarians and chair of the AASL Task Force on Leadership Development. Ann is the recipient of the 2011 AASL National School Library Media Program of the Year Award for the district; the 2002 AASL National School Library Media Program of the Year Award for an individual school; Longwood University Professionals Who Made a Difference Award, 2008; Virginia Tech "Excellence in Education Award," 2000; Gale's DISCovering Excellence in Education Award, 1998; Phi Delta Kappa Chapter 1431 "Outstanding Teacher Award," 1991; and Virginia Education Association's "Peace and International Relations Award," 1991. Ann is author of *Seven Steps to an Award-Winning School Library Program* (Libraries Unlimited, 2012).

David Schuster, MLS, has been working in school library automation for 20 years. He is an AASL affiliate member, Texas Association of School Librarian—Councilor (TASL), and serves on several committees in TLA (Texas Library Association), including the Shirley Igo School Library PTA Collaboration Award committee. Former leadership roles include chair of Texas Association of School Librarian Administrators (TASLA, 2007), CODI Users Group president (2005), TALL Texan Leadership Institute (2010), and currently president of the Frisco Public Library Foundation in Frisco, Texas (since 1999). He is an adjunct at the University of North Texas in the College of Information with the School Library Program (2010).

Roz Thompson is currently the teacher-librarian and student learning coordinator at Tumwater High School in Tumwater, Washington. She has been a school librarian for eight years and had the pleasure to spend one of those years as an elementary school librarian. Prior to that, she taught English, math, and social studies at the high school level. She has served as legislative chair for the Washington Library Media Association for the past five years. Roz graduated with a master's in education from the University of Washington and with a BA in history from Whitman College.